DO NOT REMOVE
CARDS FROM POCKET

STARTING AT
THE TOP

STARTING AT THE TOP

America's New Achievers:
Twenty-three Success Stories
Told by Men and Women Whose
Dreams of Being Boss Came True

JOHN MACK CARTER
and JOAN FEENEY

William Morrow and Company, Inc.

New York

Library of Congress Cataloging in Publication Data

Carter, John Mack.
Starting at the top.

Includes index.
1. Businessmen—United States—Biography.
2. Entrepreneur. 3. Success in business—United States—
Case studies. I. Feeney, Joan. II. Title.
HC102.5.A2C37 1985   338'.04'0922 [B]   85-4826
ISBN 0-688-04520-0

Printed in the United States of America

First Edition

1 2 3 4 5 6 7 8 9 10
BOOK DESIGN BY ELLEN LO GIUDICE

CONTENTS

INTRODUCTION

Success stories are not about ideas or inventions. They are about people. Take any example of self-made success—in this book or anywhere in the world—and you can trace it back to people determined to do whatever it was they set out to do. Their success is not dependent upon the products or services they provide. They would have succeeded in almost any endeavor—except climbing the traditional corporate ladder.

That ladder has itself become outdated. No longer do we identify business success with the pyramid of managers and executives within giant corporations. The eighties is the age of the entrepreneur. *Starting at the Top* documents this shift in business and the national consciousness. It looks beyond the corporate suite and hardscrabble climb of the seventies and investigates the successes of today, those individuals who, by choosing to work for themselves, elected to start at the *top*.

To call this change in orientation new is somewhat misleading. It is, of course, the revitalization of the familiar American dream, only now it is all sense and no sentimentality. Opportunity was for two centuries synonymous with America, the place where anyone who had the dream and the determination could achieve unlimited goals.

After World War II, however, we began to glorify the marvel of mass production and the corporate chiefs who managed it, the men—rarely the women—who advanced steadily through the crowded ranks to the rarefied air of the executive tower. They were the public heroes of the fifties and sixties, models for us all.

But as big businesses grew even bigger, many became encumbered by their very size, by the imperative for continual growth. Managers took over from builders. Financial officers gained control of what the founders and producers had built, assets were "managed," profits were "maximized," and staffs were "reorganized" by management consultants. The chiefs became caretakers of what others had made. The business of America faltered, and confidence in business leaders sagged. Corporate chiefs no longer represented the height of attainment.

Opinion polls reflected this collapse of trust and respect. The public sensed that corporations had removed themselves from the people they served, and people became disaffected with impersonal and often inefficient corporate products and services. What had happened to our national pride in the *Fortune* 500? Where was the daring and imagination that had made America great? Many capable executives who realized how limited their control ultimately was began to be disturbed by the question, Is this all there is?

Enter the entrepreneurs. They are themselves generally disillusioned with the corporate culture, their confidence and respect are in themselves, and their interests lie in *better* rather than simply more. In short, they don't want to be the CEO of the company, they want to be the company.

Starting at the Top looks toward both the future and the past: By considering the future path of American success—entrepreneurism—it conjures up the personalities of the original American success stories, the Woolworths and the Fords and the Carnegies. Entrepreneurs have always been with us. They faded from prominence for a while, but they are again in ascendency. About six hundred thousand new businesses will be started this year, six times the average start-up rate during the fifties. Since 1976 the number of self-employed people has risen 28 percent, with over nine million people working for themselves in 1983. In this book we look at some of these entrepreneurs.

Starting at the Top is the view from inside the winner's circle. It tells the stories and provides the insights that textbooks can't because these lessons don't translate into formulas and charts. The almost two dozen people in this book discuss their insights, progress, choices, and luck, and the result is a collective profile of the eighties achievers in their own words. Their ambitions and backgrounds are wonderfully varied. We begin at the beginning: How did Nolan Bushnell happen to invent Atari? How did David Brown go from journalism to producing *Jaws* and *The Verdict*? How did Helen Boehm become head of America's foremost porcelain company? Why did David Liederman give up a law practice to start David's Cookies? And then we look to the future: how the entrepreneurs handle and manage their success.

The entrepreneurs don't talk about organization charts and theories; they talk about hard times and good luck. They haven't studied advanced management, and their marketing is usually common sense. They haven't been promoted by performance reviews, but are self-elected. They started out as individuals with perceptions of customer needs and the determination to do it themselves—not necessarily in that order. And, finally, since there are no safety nets, they succeed largely because they can't afford to fail.

There is much disagreement among the people in this book. Probably the only point on which everyone agrees is that there is no formula for success. There is no advice which, even if followed exactly, is guaranteed to produce results. For this reason, instead of distilling the experience and wisdom of those who have succeeded into ten or a hundred rules of "how to succeed," what we offer here are the stories and illustrations of what these people *did*—and why it did or didn't work. *Starting at the Top* is a popular encyclopedia of the new success.

The book is organized around those issues that keep coming up in any discussion of success. (Success, like most things, looks much easier with the help of hindsight: progress appears more linear, decisions wiser, and success itself almost inevitable.) Rather than presenting each person's story in its entirety, we have broken up the interviews by topic: getting started, expectations, goals, breakthroughs, personality, growth, business practices, and so on. What this book does is orchestrate a dialogue among these many voices so that common themes and disagreements, shared problems and unique solutions, universal traits and personal quirks emerge. The result is the complete success profile.

Starting at the Top is not just the bright side of success—the money and the accolades that come with it—but rather it's about the *process,* the *getting* there as well as the there.

The people in this book were selected for their success as judged by the common standards of fortune and fame. Some names are well known, others are still emerging, and a few are even sliding down the other side of the summit. All have this in common: They are self-made. Through determination, commitment, luck, and a sense of humor, they have accomplished what they set out to do.

Our choices also reflect contemporary trends in American business. People who have excelled in computers, video games, food services, and consulting are here, as are representatives from advertising, film production, manufacturing, apparel design, marketing, education, publishing, and medicine, among others.

Many more interviews were conducted than appear in

this volume, just as only the most relevant or revealing remarks made by an individual are included. All aspects of success are covered, from the nuts and bolts of financing (and the myriad different approaches to it) to sophisticated views of marketing.

Each story is told in the language of experience. In explaining how innovations come about, for example, restaurateur George Lang talks about finding new desserts; management consultant John Diebold speaks in terms of corporate change; designer Milton Glaser discusses getting around obstacles, Richard LaMotta talks about selling his Chipwiches from pushcarts. What they have in common is passion. Their immersion in whatever they're doing is so complete that their careers become their vantage point for viewing the world.

Most of the people we talked to are too busy pursuing their success to have spent much time reflecting on its nature. Our goal was to lead them into doing something they rarely do: separate themselves from their success and look at what they do from a broader perspective than their appointment calendars afford. We asked what success means, what it takes, what it costs. Often we were told that this was the first time they had ever stopped to consider their success in that way. And so, we believe, this is the first time that anyone has presented an account of success for the eighties.

These are the stories of how success happens in America.

I. MEET THE
ENTREPRENEURS

Twelve short, concise, and highly diverse first-person stories of how success was achieved

Some plotted out a business-school approach, some took advantage of chance occurrences, and still others relied on common sense alone. No matter what the route taken, however, each of these stories is a story of how someone got his or her start and made good from there.

The range of fields and achievements and methods indicates that there is no such thing as a formula for success, although there do emerge from these tales certain guiding principles and important lessons.

These are the stories of how success happens in America.

YOU HAVE TO GET A SHTICK

Richard Leibner, N. S. BIENSTOCK, INC., TELEVISION NEWS TALENT AGENCY

I started out as a CPA. Nate Bienstock, who originally created the business, sold insurance to and did tax work for lots of people in the publishing business. Nate Bienstock became a legend in his own time. He started as an industrial-insurance salesman, going door to door selling life insurance for a quarter, a week or a month at a time. He met another insurance agent who said,

"You have to have a style, you have to have a gimmick, you have to have a shtick," and he hyped Nate. This guy put him in the direction of finding a groove and a following.

In the late thirties, early forties, Nate began to hang around the halls at Time-Life, CBS. Income taxes had just become something you couldn't do in two minutes, and Nate was always a hustler. Communications became his hook.

So Nate begins to make all of these connections, and then the war starts and a lot of the group goes off to cover the war, and Nate says, "Look, you've got emergencies, I'll take care of things, even pay the bills for you while you're gone." If you bought a life-insurance policy from Nate Bienstock, and he made a commission, he'd carry you to Forty-second Street on his back.

Getting a Specialty

So Nate gets a specialty. Some of the guys begin to come back from the war, and television news starts and a bunch of them say to Nate, "Represent us." He's just a savvy, nice man who paid the bills, wrote them life insurance, did their tax work, and knew trustworthy lawyers. By this time, Nate had become one of the top insurance salesmen in America, over a million dollars a year. So Nate starts representing them and he has about twenty-five clients, no contracts. He's collecting 3 percent on each.

Nate understood that television was coming of age, and he knew that the news was going to begin to happen. In 1965 Nate was in his sixties. His health wasn't good and he started to look for somebody to sell the business to. Nate knew my father, a CPA. Nate had had a high blood pressure attack and he said, "I've got to go away for three or four weeks. Can you help service this thing?"

I had at this time already made the big mistake. I had

wanted to be what my father was, a CPA. I had been brought up that way. I got sucked in—like father, like son. My father's health was beginning to suffer, and my mother laid a guilt trip on me: "Come to work for Dad." I went to work for my father, which was the best move and the worst move I ever made in my life. You shouldn't work for a parent. Period.

I was now back over a year and I was beginning to hate accounting; there was nothing creative. I was about ready to go drive a cab.

So I went to this dinner with Nate. We worked out a way that I would give it a half a day every day for the two months he was away. We shook hands that if I really liked it, we'd come back and my father would make a deal with him to form a corporation and find some way to go into the business.

We set up the deal on an hourly basis, and I filled in while Nate went away. I didn't love the job; I was clearing paychecks, doing nothing. But suddenly news became something to me. There was a list of thirty-five names—who were they? What did they look like? Who was Eric Sevareid? Winston Burdett? Alexander Kendrick? Jules Bergman? Lou Cioffi? Nate had a lot of the early best names; he paid Walter Cronkite's bills. I started watching news on two sets, and I became totally enamored of it. When Nate talked about how it had to grow and become important, I believed him.

We made a buy-out deal with Nate over a number of years. Our first year in business N. S. Bienstock, Inc. grossed $48,000. I had to get a life-insurance license; I had to play the game and help support the office. But I began to wrap into the news business. I made my father keep his promise. So I'm out of the accounting office and the news is my business. Now I didn't have to worry about how big a raise I gave someone or wasting my time on lunches and that kind of stuff.

The business began to grow like crazy.

IT'S NOT THE PRODUCT, IT'S THE PROMOTION

Jeffrey Feinman, PRESIDENT, VENTURA ASSOCIATES, PROMOTIONAL CONSULTANTS

I had a theory that if you look at product selling in this country, it's gone through phases. First, you made the best chair in the world and the world beat a path to your door. Then, through technology, anybody could make a chair; today, a good organic chemist and two hundred dollars will tell you how to make any product chemically. Next it became the best advertising. After you got to parity products, you got to parity advertising: eleven full-page ads for cigarettes in *TV Guide.* I perceived that the next step was promotion—the ten thousand-dollar prize you could tell a consumer he or she might already have won to get them into the gas station. *That* was what was going to make the marketing difference.

I saw the promotion business as a real opportunity business because it was characterized by a lot of guys who just hadn't made it anywhere else. If you didn't know what to do with your idiot son-in-law, you made him the sales-promotion manager and put him in charge of the slide projector. Today there are still companies like that.

The sales-promotion business got hot, and a lot of people in it got rich because big companies started to think it was a good investment. Procter & Gamble started spending more money in promotion dollars than in ad dollars.

DEFINE YOUR PURPOSE

David Liederman, FOUNDER, "DAVID'S COOKIES"

• The basic business philosophy I have, somebody in the magazine business told me. The guy told me, A lot of people have crazy ideas for new magazines, and if you cannot, in your own mind, define the purpose of your magazine idea *in one sentence,* you don't know what the hell you're talking about. It's the same thing with any kind of business concept.

The philosophy is, whatever business you go into, do it better than anybody else and charge for it. This covers both ends: It protects the customer and it protects you. We make it better and we charge for it.

The Cardinal Rule: Give the Public a Good Product

Value for money, that's the bottom line. You don't forget the cardinal rule: You don't cheat the public. You give them a good product.

Anybody who wants to make money in the food business has to wake up to the fact that you have to give the public value for money. The game is over where—unless you're McDonald's—you can convince a supposedly unsuspecting public to go eat something by jamming advertising down their throats.

An example? Pringle's potato chips. People won't buy them anymore. When they started the product, they spent about $130 million in new product development just to get the thing off the ground, and they backed it up with a lot of advertising. But the public wouldn't buy because it was a bad product.

So, what's happening is that there are a number of small companies, like David's Cookies and Häagen-Dazs, that are giving people a better product and charging them for it.

The my-daddy-is-bigger-than-your-daddy syndrome in the food business only goes so far. David's has the best cookies. I can look you in the eye and tell you that because nobody's using better ingredients than I am. Häagen-Dazs *is* the best ice cream because nobody is using better ingredients and mixing their ice cream better than that. And there are very few products that can make that claim.

We've gotten where we are with basically no advertising—we may have put fifteen or twenty thousand dollars *total* in advertising since we started—and we're opening stores at the rate of two a week. So something is happening out there.

DO IT BETTER AND CHARGE FOR IT

Dr. Richard Winter, FOUNDER, EXECUTIVE HEALTH
EXAMINERS

We started with the idea that you could not get a really comprehensive medical examination in the city of New York (which was where we started) done decently where you were treated like a human being, get in and get out and have it all under one roof, at a fair price, with good doctors, done properly. It didn't exist. This was in 1959.

At that time there was a clinic that was seeing a very large number of people a year for cancer checkups, at $25 per person. So I thought, if that clinic can see 20,000 people a year at $25 apiece, I'm going to open a cancer clinic and I'm going to charge $50 apiece, but I'm going to do it much nicer and much better and see 3,000 to 4,000 a year. The reason I'm going to get patients is that someone is willing to spend a little more to get better care in nicer surroundings.

So I talked to some business people about it, and one executive said to me, "Dr. Winter, you're wrong. What you need is the whole-man concept. Executives, and those are the people you're talking to, are not just interested in cancer. They're interested in their hearts and their blood pressure as well as cancer, and you really ought to do everything."

I decided that he was probably right. I decided I was going to do that.

SATISFYING YOUR CUSTOMER

Jeffrey Hollender, FOUNDER AND PRESIDENT, NETWORK FOR LEARNING, ADULT EDUCATION

Right now, because of the shift in demographics—the population in America is getting older and older—everybody wants to get into adult education. They all want to move in and be competitive and offer adult-education classes.

One of the biggest problems is that their orientation is somewhat backward. Their orientation when you sign up for the class is, *We're* going to grade *you* and then *we're* going to give *you* a degree and then you can walk away happy and that's what you get for your money. That doesn't work in noncredit adult-education programs. It's just the opposite. You're going to come in and spend money and then *you're* going to grade *me*. You're going to ask, "How good was that course, how good was that teacher, how comfortable was I, did the class start on time, and am I willing to pay them any more money to learn anything again?" Most people in education don't understand that. They don't treat their students like customers. People who are in the retail business understand that a little better. People who are selling products understand that.

Selling One Idea Several Ways

We also have a line of audio cassettes that Walden Books markets nationally, and we have a joint venture with Warner Amex in which we're producing a number of television shows for the home-video market—informationally oriented as opposed to educationally oriented shows.

Everything we do has the same direction. The activities we're involved in are all based on software. They're all based on the concept that the core of our business is the core of what Procter & Gamble's business is: developing things and products that people want to buy, knowing how to sell it to them, how to price it, and how to package it. In that sense we approach education the way anyone intelligently approaches any product as a business. We combine research with a bit of creativity and intelligent marketing techniques. What we do is package information.

TAKE ONE IDEA AND EXPAND ON IT

Nolan Bushnell, FOUNDER, ATARI, PIZZA TIME THEATRE, CATALYST TECHNOLOGIES

What I was doing before and what I'm doing now are exactly the same. I started out as a systems engineer. I built systems that worked on resistors and transistors and integrated circuits. Then I turned it into running a company, Atari, that built systems. And now I've built another system and this system is designed to make companies. It's all a matter of systems analysis. Building systems is just changing your Tinkertoy set.

Forging into New Areas

I've always tried to be in the forefront, forging strategies in new areas. Once we had the coin-operated-machine business pretty much under control, I was pushing into the consumer-electronics business. Once the consumer games were fixed, we were pushing into the consumer-programming business. Once the consumer thing was going, we got into the personal-computer market. I always knew we were being aggressive but I always felt that each new thing was within the capability of the company.

Vertical Expansion

I felt for a long time that I wanted control of the environment in which the Atari games were used. I felt that a significant number of the games were going into locations that were not acceptable. I wanted to be in the operations side of the business as well as the manufacturing side. For revenues, too. I wanted to be able to be in that business without giving all my money to the location because, traditionally, game centers had to be in high-traffic locations, which are very, very expensive pieces of real estate. I said, "I don't want to play that game. I want the world to come to me." Why are they going to come to me? Well, I'm going to provide them with food as well as entertainment. What kind of entertainment? Well, let's do entertainment that I can control. Let's provide them with "technology" entertainment. Why not robots?

Pizza Time Theatre was started inside Atari, and after Warner bought Atari they sold the Pizza Time concept back to me. We started the Pizza Time concept at an amusement trade show. We bought a costume, a walk-around costume that was being sold to amusement parks. We took it home to our engineers, threw it at them and said, "Hey, make it talk." Hired a guy to do a business plan for the restaurant business, wrote some plans, and built one. And that was the prototype. Then we started building one every five days.

Almost along with the Pizza Time thing came opportunities to fund two or three other businesses, robots and things. And so I started funding some of those other items as a venture capitalist.

It seemed like every time I'd fund one of those, they'd go through some of the same inefficient start-up hassles.

"Which attorney do I see? What Xerox machine do I buy? What telephone system should I install? How many square feet should I rent? Do I need a financial guide yet? Who should I use for accountants?" All the same old stuff. So I decided I wanted to make it so that a company could be formed quickly and efficiently. I wanted to institutionalize some of the things I had learned about the formation process, all the way from patent law to antitrust law to how to keep your books and how to market your product.

Profit Motive

We are motivated by greed. We believe that knowledge is power, and we believe that putting smart people in an environment in which the mistakes are minimized can be an extremely powerful concept for success.

I want to manage assets, and this is the best way I can think of for what I want to do. I cannot be one of the people who helps fund PG&E or Detroit Edison. That represents a certain conservative risk-reward profile that's really nice for widows and orphans. I'm a technologist, I like to roll. I want something that has a high opportunity. I want to do a hundred times on my money.

When I say I want to manage assets, I want that to be a broad concept. I consider good people assets, I feel that good ideas are assets, I feel that money is an asset. I want to really make sure that these things click and work together efficiently and capably.

TURNING AN AVOCATION INTO A VOCATION

Otto Bettmann, FOUNDER, THE BETTMANN ARCHIVE

The Archive is rather a very strange fusion of European scholarship and American practical ability. When

I came here from Germany, I despised money and I did not intend to go into business. I was thirty-five, I was a scholar, I was connected with museums, lectures, books.

I had, however, a spark of an idea that struck me when I was in one of the large libraries in Berlin, in charge of rare books, incunabula, that one could build up a picture collection, not according to artist—Botticelli or van Gogh and so on—but according to subject: music, watchmaking, and so on. In my day-to-day work, people always asked me for article subjects. They wanted to illustrate a cookbook or a fashion book, or a doctor wanted to write a book about artificial teeth or something. So I built up a collection in a cigar box of things that went from *A* to *Z*, from abacus to zymosis, and had this all arranged.

My father was a doctor, but he really started me in this business. I collected pictures from his wastepaper basket. The pharmaceutical firms sent him all sorts of advertisements with old pictures of doctors and pharmacies, and I was always fascinated by it. I assembled these and later on I expanded. It was more or less an avocation of a historian. I did not think of it as a living, a life-sustaining thing. I pictured myself more as a museum curator.

When I came to America there was this idea that America was not interested in the historical, the dusty-musty. I found it just the opposite, that there's an incredible interest in backgrounds for the very reason that we here in America do not have this broad historical background that Europeans have. Our history is short and we have to underbuild it with some sort of reference to the past: in a way, to give our existence a third dimension. In Europe it exists already.

I came here with this collection and I started looking for university connections, for my whole background and all my aspirations were really more scholarly than commercmercial.

mercial. I came at a very propitious moment, for this was a time when American journalism and the whole communications field turned toward the visual, the early time of *Life* magazine and *Look* and all of those. I simply was swept along on this wave of pictorial journalism. All of a sudden the publishers found out that I was here. It turned out to be a fairly profitable business, for after all, the principle is rather sound. It so happens that once we have a picture, we can use it again and again.

In a way yet, I think of myself primarily as a scholar.

THE BUSINESS OF NEW IDEAS AND INNOVATION

John Diebold, FOUNDER AND PRESIDENT, THE DIEBOLD GROUP, INC., MANAGEMENT CONSULTANTS

My position has always been that the people who've made the biggest errors in trying to compete with IBM, for example, have been the people who held up a mirror to IBM and tried to copy the image. They played IBM's game in IBM's court by IBM's rules (and they obviously lost)—instead of looking at themselves and figuring out what their own strengths and weaknesses were, what the market and the opportunities were, and what *they* could do. All the successes have been of this kind—where they've tried to assess the uniqueness of their own positions and worked on that, rather than copying a leader.

A very important function of ours is providing a totally independent reading of a situation. Today, computers and automation play a vital role in many companies, and thousands of people are dealing with them, and one of the things we often do is review their efficiency: Are they applying them toward the right ends? Are they simply mechanizing yesterday's business, or are they really trying to do new things by using the technologies, and are they using them on things that count?

There are many things you can do that are very time consuming and don't really count. You can put activities on a computer and it takes a lot of effort and time to do it, and it might or might not save some money, but it isn't really going to make much difference to the business. Providing independent readings on this sort of thing is very important because companies get an array of proposals from suppliers and they don't know which ones to choose. They get a lot of internal proposals from departments that are protecting themselves, and the problem is for somebody to come in and view it and try to give an unbiased position. Our career isn't dependent on how well we handle other people in the company. We're being judged on the question of giving the best advice. So those things, as well as new ideas, are what we bring.

Producing Something Quite New

I'm very interested in how you can change the parameters of competition by using some of these technologies. Today they are mostly used to mechanize the routine functions in business. I think that what's interesting is where you can deliver. In publishing, for example, you may have a financial analyst using three or four different directories to try to do an analysis. Well, if as publisher you're able to put a terminal in the analyst's office and let him draw and ask original questions and get original answers drawn from several data bases, tailored to fit his questions, he can go through a train of questions and answers in an afternoon and thus save two months of work.

I think if I ran McGraw-Hill, that's how I'd compete, through producing a new service—not putting the publication out on a television set, but producing something quite new. I've always been very interested in that.

MAKING CONNECTIONS

Jerry Rubin, FOUNDER, BUSINESS NETWORKING SALONS

I come from need, personal need. I believe that if you act out of your personal need, you touch the needs of thousands, maybe even millions, because we're all the same.

My need was twofold. I was separated from my wife at the time, and I wanted to meet a lot of women who were interesting and substantial. I believe in doing things as efficiently as possible; I don't have the time to meet one person a week, I have to meet ten a night. So I thought to myself, the best way to meet people is through friends and I guess I could call up my friends and say, "Introduce me to somebody." But that's time consuming, and why would anybody do it? So I said, "I have a better idea. I'll invite my friends to bring the most interesting person they know to my house." So I just turned it around, used some imagination with the need.

The second thing about my need was that I was the marketing director of an investment-banking house, and I wanted to meet a lot of financially leveraged people very quickly. We were financing companies; I wanted to meet a lot of potential entrepreneurs, potential investors, people with great ideas.

Serendipity

I thought I was looking for ideas. Little did I know that my vehicle was going to become the idea. I'm a great believer in serendipity: That is, you set a goal for yourself and you never achieve the goal, but another goal appears along the way that is even better, one you never would have thought of because it is too unusual or out of the ordinary.

I didn't know when I started the salons that they would become the business. I thought the business would be meeting someone at the salon and then going off on an idea—solar energy, health food stores, whatever it was. It turned out that the salon itself became the idea.

This all happened because I connected my needs to a market. There was a market out there of people like myself, who wanted to meet business people and members of the opposite sex and who wanted to make friends, too. Some come for sex and end up making money, some come to make money and end up getting married.

The Network began to turn into a business when I noticed how many people of high quality were coming and somebody came to me and said, "You ought to make this a business." He was representing a discotheque and he was suggesting I have a big party at the discotheque. So I thought to myself, "Well, I guess the people I'm now attracting to my apartment are not going to go on a regular basis to this particular disco, but perhaps there is another group of people who are equally interesting, but different, who would be interested. So let's give it a try." So I gave it a try and it was fantastic: 2,500 people, lines around the block, the biggest night in the history of that particular place. And at that point I said, "I have a talent here."

WORKING WITH THINGS THAT YOU KNOW

Christopher Whittle, CHAIRMAN, *ESQUIRE* MAGAZINE

My partner, Phillip Moffit, and I launched a thing called *Nutshell* as a local college magazine when we were students, and we published it to make money during school. Actually, the way it began was we were running the orientation programs for the university for all incoming students. There were so many students coming in that it was impossible to really give them any kind of attention, so we said maybe we should do a magazine for them. That's where we got the idea. We started the magazine, and then we decided that we would do it at every major university in the country, because the response was so good at that one school. We ultimately were publishing 115 different local magazines around the United States, rather than one national magazine, and this was a mammoth undertaking. It was a real trial by fire to try to put that together and make it work.

It wasn't solely or principally a money-making enterprise: We were very interested in students at the time, which was 1969, and all of us who started it were student leaders. We've always published for our peers. That's been a key: We've worked out of things that we knew. And we knew about students—a lot.

We didn't *say*, "Let's do things that we know how to do." I think it did sneak up on us. We have gravitated naturally towards doing things we understand. If we understand them, we do them better. *Esquire* is definitely a publication for our peers. We were twenty-eight years old and though our student-publication business was doing wonderfully and was the best in its field, the students were not our peers anymore and we turned it over to people who *are* peers of those readers. We staffed it with intern groups from colleges, so that it is still a peer publishing operation.

We do sixteen magazines, so clearly not every one of them is for our peers, but it has been the thread. I think it's really contributed to our success.

A BUSINESS-SCHOOL APPROACH

John DePasquale, FOUNDER AND PRESIDENT, THE DM
GROUP, DIRECT MARKETING

Strengths and Weaknesses

While I was going to the Wharton business school, I saw a publication for MBAs. It was then the thesis project of a few fellows up at the Harvard business school. I ended up meeting them in New York when I joined Arthur Young and they joined other companies. I said I would consult with them free in marketing and consumer behavior, and who knows—maybe the magazine would work. It occurred to me that if the publication really worked, it might be the entrepreneurial venture I was looking for.

So for two years I worked full-time at Arthur Young and part-time at the magazine. I was their circulation director, data-processing director, and research director. The scary moment came when we felt it was big enough to support four or five people; we all quit our other jobs and took serious cuts in pay, and any money that we did end up making we plowed back into the company. After I was with the venture five months, the economy began to turn bad: Paper prices shot up, postage shot up, client budgets began to dry up. We had numerous worries. I said to my partners, "You folks continue to try to confront this problem of rising costs and sliding revenues, and let me think about what we have, who we are, what our strengths and weaknesses are, and see if we can confront this issue indirectly or obliquely and maybe do something we weren't planning on." That's how we got into research.

I said, "What is happening is, a lot of people—banks, corporations, insurance companies, accounting firms—are hiring MBAs by the droves. Let's undertake a survey of all the schools and publish a research vehicle about MBA recruiting practices—who does them well, who does them poorly, what the recruits think, what the starting salaries are at various schools, and so on." We distilled some of the information to the students so they could prepare themselves for the process, but we sold volumes of the information and studies to the recruiters, so recruiters could take a look at what the competition was.

Know What Business You're In

That taught me lesson one: Know what business you're in. All along we thought we were in the magazine business, but it became clear to me that we weren't. We were in the publishing business. We kept the magazine, but we began to publish these research reports. And every six months we included in our publication a distillation of this information for the student. So I learned lesson two: leverage. Everything you do, try to sell three ways if you can.

When a problem is confronting you, look broader, don't look more narrowly. Therefore, from the magazine business we looked more broadly into the publishing business, and publishing got us into research.

Converting Difficulties into Assets

Over the last ten years I have realized that one thing that makes my style of management and way of doing things different is that I have a vision of how to take an adversary difficulty and convert it into a positive. But at the same time, I also love the implementation. I'm not the visionary dreamer. I am the kind of person who can envision and then roll up my sleeves and get it done. I get a real charge out of results, not out of dreams. That is why, I am certain, I gravitated to the business of direct response, direct marketing; it is so absolutely measurable, targetable, challenging, and result-oriented every day of the week.

Know Your Market

Problem number two came: The costs kept going up. So we integrated again, and got into brochure publishing. Not only did we ask "What business are we in?" but we forced the decision, "Who is our market?" At one point we were confused. We were thinking our market was the reader, and that's true if you're in the magazine business, but the fact of the matter was, the market was not only the reader but also the corporations that were looking to recruit that reader, the corporations that were buying our books. We said, "Let's go to them and publish the recruitment vehicle that they send to the campuses and the about-to-graduate MBAs read before the recruiters come." So we got into the on-campus-brochure-writing creative production business. This leveraged our editorial and our creative staffs, our paper-buying and printing capabilities. It wasn't that much quantity still, but twice as much of nothing is a pretty good handful.

The downfall of a lot of entrepreneurs is that they don't separate their love of what they're doing from the activity that lets them keep doing it, which is anything making money. A lot of entrepreneurs are not successful because they can't see the forest for the trees. It's like you get married to a stock and you watch it go down to zero.

When the basic business has changed and is no good anymore, you should cut it off and start to expand those peripheral businesses—peripheral in that they're the ones you just started. But we didn't do that, so we were publishing the brochures, we were publishing the research reports, and we were doing nothing to try to improve the mother lode, which was the magazine. The problems kept mounting, and all we were able to do was slow the slide.

Focusing On the Problem

It kept going, and I said, "One of the reasons we're having problems getting more advertising is that advertisers say, 'How do I know my advertising in your publication is doing me any good?' " We couldn't give the answer to that. So I focused on that problem, and that's how I got into direct mail.

The solution to the problem was figuring out a way of tracing that. I went to the advertisers in the magazine. The first advertiser I went to—I'll never forget it—was Coolidge Bank and Trust, in Watertown, Massachusetts. We did an American Express Gold Card program with Coolidge, and mailed it to the second-year MBA class at Harvard. We had about a 70 percent response to the mailing, which was outrageous. Exactly what I was looking for. I loved it, because we had a success and it was demonstrable without question.

I went back to the bank and they wanted to do more immediately. Over the course of a year, we took the program nationwide. We actually broke down the barriers to banking: This little bank had customers in almost all fifty states, because those MBAs graduated and took off.

I went back to my partners and said, "Guys, the answer to our problem is that we should become a direct-mail, direct-marketing company that publishes magazines, not a magazine company that does direct mail." This is where the entrepreneur's love of the business starts to get in his way of objective decision making. My partners were magazine folk, born and bred. Though the solution was obvious to me, it was not nearly so obvious to them, not because I was smarter but because I have the ability to be objective; I learned through life the value of a certain detachment.

To be successful, you also have to have some lucky breaks. But you have to be insightful enough to know when a break is lucky. In 1971 American Express called up and said, "We see the number of gold cards this little Coolidge Bank is extending, growing by comparison to Chembank and Bankers Trust—banks many times the size of Coolidge. What's going on?" Then American Express said, "Could you write us a proposal to do the same for a few of our other banks?"

American Express wanted to do it in three or four banks. I wrote a proposal for all two hundred banks. They bought it. The thing that was nice was now we had assured income. The Coolidge bank was great but they were one client; American Express represented two hundred clients with only one place to bill. Plus it let me get into all those banks. So we were slowly building the business and I loved it.

Banking presents a tremendous opportunity in direct marketing, because back in those days there was really no such thing as bank marketing as we know it today; Banking was a homogeneous product and a checking account a checking account. So here was an opportunity to become active in a major industry. I liked the industry because banks, in my vision then, make money good times and bad—we didn't know then that bank failures would happen like they are today. I knew I wasn't going to have too many accounts-receivable problems; if you deal with a Chase or a Citibank, you're going to get paid.

Getting In on the Ground Floor

It all made sense to me, and, most importantly, I saw an opportunity as the industry of direct marketing was growing. In the mid-sixties direct mail wasn't even an industry at all, if you forget the Sears Roebuck, Montgomery Ward catalogs. So we were going to get in on the ground floor of an industry. I knew that we weren't alone in our insight and that others were going to see the opportunity and therefore I figured if we concentrated on an industry—banking—that nobody was paying attention to, we'd be left to grow sight unseen while the competition was trying to knock the door down at General Foods.

So I went back again to my partners and said, "Really, this is right. Not only can I feel it, but it's proven here. Look at what we're making, look at what we're losing."

When they still wouldn't give up the magazine, I said, This is not for me. We didn't have enough ability, or resources, to build a magazine business. We were in competition with Hearst and everybody else, whereas in the direct-mail business we were in competition with nobody.

I decided that I definitely had found, at least at this juncture in my life, what I wanted to do—direct marketing. So I set about leaving.

The next three years were spent methodically building a direct-mail business. Basically what the DM Group was at the time was a direct-mail agency. We went to a client, let's say a bank that wanted to generate more credit card customers. We would write the marketing plan, we would then write the copy, design the package, using all free-lance people and keeping overhead low. I kept learning from past experience, building a future, as opposed to a present. I set about not just selling jobs, but cultivating clients and understanding the business. I would recommend that anybody do that, trade off the immediate business to build a stronger base.

SOMETHING NEW AND UNIQUE

Jan Stuart, FOUNDER, JAN STUART NATURAL SKIN CARE FOR MEN

I felt that I had to do something nobody else was doing, something different. Be creative, work hard, I told myself, and sooner or later it will happen.

One day I was sitting at dinner with my family. My mom mentioned she had read something about men's fashion getting big, and men's fragrances, and how now the big thing is going to be men's skin care. I laughed, I laughed, I laughed. I thought it was really funny, but that's how it actually started.

The idea of skin care was not necessarily exciting. But the idea of doing something that nobody else did was. People say, "I'd love to find something that nobody else does. I'd love to find a business to go into." The hardest part is trying to find out what you want to do, and doing it.

I realized that, hey, this was a stepping stone. Getting in! If I get into the skin-care business, something new and unique, it's a stepping stone to going in other directions.

II. INSIDE SUCCESS

What does it mean, what is it worth? Feelings about fame, fortune, and satisfaction from inside the winner's circle

There seems to be no consensus on success—on what it means, on what it's worth. Just as there are innumerable ways to achieve it, there are as many ways to view it, the most common being ambivalently.

The idea of success seems to change as one approaches more closely. Many of the subjects of these "success stories" even deny that they've achieved success, and say that it is something for which they are still waiting. Some emphasize goals or motives, advantages or drawbacks. The major theme that emerges is that, contrary to popular supposition, success does not automatically bring satisfaction.

The other major concern voiced is simply, What next? "Success" is not enough.

WHAT IT TAKES TO FEEL SATISFIED

Lois Wyse, CO-FOUNDER, WYSE ADVERTISING

I'm Never Satisfied

Success is a very funny word. I still don't feel "successful." I look around and there isn't any place that I

36

look that someone isn't brighter, richer, further ahead of me in business, more talented, prettier—so I don't feel successful.

I think I'll be successful when I look around and can't find anyone who does it better than I do. That's what keeps me going. I'm never satisfied. I only want to be better.

Richard Leibner, AGENT

Being the Best

ɾ So many people have the compulsion to say success is *this* much. To me, success is your reputation—even if it was only fleeting. If at any time you achieve the pinnacle of quality in what you pursue, that's the greatest satisfaction. Having the money to eat doesn't hurt. People get mad at me: "You do too much." But there's never enough. And it's not the money. It's the inertia of the thing.

Jeffrey Feinman, PROMOTIONAL CONSULTANT

ɾ I don't feel successful. I am my own harshest critic. Certainly success is not any amount of money to me. It's finding worthwhile goals and working at them. If it's money you want, I don't think it's hard to be successful.

John DePasquale, DIRECT MARKETING

There's a Reason

ɾ My goal all along was to make a contribution to the world, somehow. I didn't know what I was going to do, but in a very simple way I figured you are put on earth for a reason and it's not just to walk through life and buy something. Find out what that reason is and then go and do it to the best of your ability. I know it might sound naïve and very trite, but it's a fact, and it's guided my life.

I still don't know what the reason is for me. I don't think it was to build a direct-mail company, but in the process of trying to find that reason, I want to be the best at what I do. The hallmark of the firm is excellence. I absolutely want to be the best there is in the business. That doesn't mean we don't make errors—we do. But fewer than most, you bet your life.

Edward McCabe, CO-FOUNDER, SCALI, McCABE, SLOVES
ADVERTISING

To me, success is being the best or among the best at what you do. At times, I have attained that. You keep setting higher goals. You get to a point within a field or an area of endeavor where you're sort of permanently in an upper tier, but that's erratic because you can't always be 100 percent at doing the thing you do.

Doing Other Things

When you achieve success at one thing for a fairly substantial period of time, then the question has to become whether you just continue to do that or do something else. I think about doing other things; I'd be foolish not to. I have all kinds of thoughts, but they're irrelevant because obviously none of them has moved me enough from what I'm doing into something else.

If you've achieved success in one field, is it challenging to achieve a similar degree of success in a field that may not be all that different? And it becomes difficult to focus on an area that's totally alien to you. Then the fear factor comes in, of course, but that has never been a factor for me because I can't find anything that interests me enough to want to do.

We sold this company five years ago for quite a bit of money, and a big-time venture-capital guy came to me and said he thought he could put together almost any deal I wanted. He said, "What would interest you?" Now at this time I was known as being one of the best copywriters in advertising, but not particularly known for management. I said, "Well, I'd like to run a computer company in Houston with eight thousand employees." He said, "Why on earth would you want to do that?" I said, "Because it's the least likely thing I could imagine I'd be qualified to do, and that would be a challenge." But ultimately that would be boring. It doesn't seem to me like a world worth conquering. I'm happy right here. It gets harder to continue doing what we do. I'm not sure ultimately that that really is enough of a challenge; on the other hand, it might be. I don't know.

The Need to Be the Best

Success is being the best at whatever it is you're doing, and I happen to be doing what I'm doing, so I devote myself to that. When I play tennis, I want to be the best, but I know I can't be. One of my problems is that if I should ever choose another area, it has to be something I believe I can be the best in. Tennis is out.

Am I good at evaluating what I'd be good at? No. That may be one of the biggest reasons for my success. I'm undaunted by the impossible.

I have never chosen a goal in my life. I never even had "being the best" as a goal until I realized I was pretty good at it. Then I began to develop a feeling that if you're going to do something, you might as well be the best at it, or try to be.

Comfort and Respect

I never aspired to be rich or famous. I'm somewhat unmoved by it. Money buys certain comforts, fame buys certain respect, but that in itself won't make the ads any better.

What I Came Here to Do

The other night a guy came up to me and said, "Your advertising on such and such account is fantastic." I knew then that the advertising was working. Again, the idea is, it should work, but when people come up to you, and say, "Boy, that's terrific advertising," that's all I came here to do. I always said, "If we do that, on a consistent basis, we'll make a lot of money." The make-a-lot-of-money part I was never really sure of. I just said that and it happened. So I proved the point. The problem now is, I don't know what the next point is to prove. Maybe that we can get to become a giant without a major deterioration in quality. I don't know of anyone who's really done that.

SUCCESS IS NOT THE GOAL

Christopher Whittle, CHAIRMAN, *ESQUIRE* MAGAZINE

Just Worry About What You're Doing

Stewart Brand had a piece in the back of the *Whole Earth Catalog* about how the *Catalog* was put together, and he talked about how you should not worry about making money. If you worry about what you're doing, the money will come. I think that's about 90 percent right. I think you have to worry about the money some, but I think you really have to worry about the other more. He had that pegged.

Helen Boehm, CO-FOUNDER, BOEHM PORCELAIN

"Success" Isn't a Goal

We didn't see Boehm as becoming a successful business—and then it just turned out that way because we had a good product, our credentials were fine, our service was excellent, our reputation was the highest.

A Purpose in Life

I have such a purpose in life; everyone should have. You have to remember, I was born in Brooklyn: from Brooklyn to Buckingham Palace, from the Greyhound to the Concorde. Anything can happen. It's how hard you dare to dream, how hard you dare to work, how hard you dare to love what you do.

In the beginning our goal was creating beautiful porcelain and surviving. I think if "success" had been my goal, I would have lost much of the excitement of creating. Today I can still love that excitement of creating and have a little ease because I don't have the financial pressure.

Mary Boone, ART DEALER

It's Total Immersion

Whenever I do something, I put myself totally into it, I totally immerse myself in the idea. I went to the Rhode Island School of Design and threw myself into being an artist. Although I came to New York with the desire to be an artist, I became an art dealer just by virtue of having a job at a gallery. Three years into that I realized I could be, at best, only a good artist, and I thought even at that time I might have the capabilities of being the best as an art dealer.

To Feel Realized

I never do anything unless I can be the best. I was never seeking financial success. And I never use finances as a measure of success. To feel pleased, to feel proud of what I do, is important to me. To feel realized.

Even when I made a commitment to being an art dealer and got totally immersed in that and opened this gallery, although it was certainly the thing I wanted to do, I don't think I realized how totally pleased I would be with it. It's only in the last year that I feel I've really started hitting my stride.

Last year marked a decade that I'd been involved with art dealing. I think it takes about that long to realize the subtleties that are being satisfied in terms of your personality by a particular occupation.

I don't think I even knew when I made a commitment to the gallery how much I would absolutely love it. Now I feel that if a computer did a very in-depth personality profile of me and then put eighty thousand questions together to determine an ideal occupation, it would come up with *art dealer* for me. When I was young I'd never even heard of art dealers.

The Bad Days

There are a lot of unpleasant things I have to do in my job—that is when you're really tested at how much you love something, when even the bad days are not difficult. I can't wait to come to work.

SATISFACTIONS NOT TO BE OVERLOOKED

Richard LaMotta, FOUNDER, CHIPWICH

Pluses and Minuses

I like the action. I didn't do it to become a millionaire. That was nice that it happened, but you can only drive one fancy car and have one nice home and eat one nice steak at a time. I did it so I would have independence and wouldn't have to worry about paying my bills. When you reduce that pressure on yourself, it lets the creativity flow.

The responsibility of being the chairman of the board

here extends far more than I ever thought. When I go out to the factory and I see those older women out there working for me, they look to me and it's—"Oh, Mr. LaMotta, how're *we* doin'?" They're dependent on me to make that thing work. You're the boss. You're *their* boss.

Jeffrey Hollender, NETWORK FOR LEARNING

Enjoying What You're Doing

One of the keys is having people you enjoy working with. I look forward to coming to work because I have people who work here who are enjoyable to spend time with.

Sure, when you succeed that's great and when you make a lot of money that's great, but the people I work with—that's probably 50 percent of my enjoyment.

John DePasquale, DIRECT MARKETING

Principal Sources of Satisfaction

Watching my people grow, watching gals come in here who were secretaries three or four years ago and today are running a million-dollar piece of business, that's fantastic. Watching excellence develop in individuals, that's where I get my greatest excitement.

I feel fortunate to have been able to do what I've done. I've had ups and downs in life myself, but I think you keep going forward. The temptation when you're successful is just to rest on your laurels. I don't think it's fair to the other people here in the company. Because the company, particularly an entrepreneur's company, is built on the image of the entrepreneur, and if people come to the company because of what they like about it, it is really a tacit endorsement of what they like about the person.

Lois Wyse, ADVERTISING EXECUTIVE

Along the Way

When I was seventeen years old, I went to work for my hometown paper, the Cleveland *Press*. Along the way, I married somebody who wanted desperately to be in business for himself, so we started an advertising shopping column. He sold it and I wrote it. He had seen one done nationally, and he thought it would be a good idea to do it locally. It was called "Wise Buys by Lois."

It produced results, and we were asked by advertisers to do a little more and a little more and before we knew it we sort of backed into the advertising business, and we opened an advertising agency in Cleveland. I have never worked in any other agency; so far as I know, I invented the business as I practice it, because I had no role models.

I lived in a state of perpetual guilt. I always felt guilty because when I was at the office I thought I should be at home and when I was home I thought I should be at the office. That lasted until my children were grown, until they didn't need me anymore on a daily basis.

Success is just staying at it and never thinking you're there. I was very unhappy much of the time that I worked because I was working during a period when women didn't work. It was very difficult; I was different from my friends. I had very painful years in my life. I didn't really want to work—I never had a great desire. I always knew I could write, which is another reason why I didn't particularly want to work.

Today I'm happy that I worked, happy that I paid my dues at an early age. But I didn't know the world was going to turn around. So I didn't have any goals. My only goal was to give my husband what he wanted and what he wanted was a wife who worked. That's what I was interested in doing: being what he wanted me to be, at least at that point in his life and mine.

David Liederman, DAVID'S COOKIES

Pride

Doing Saucier, my earlier food venture, was an invaluable experience. I wish the company had done better. I'm probably more proud of the fact that it's still on the market than I am about the cookies. The thing about Saucier is, I invented that product; it was something that came out of my own *mishegaas,* my own craziness. The cookies I just took—it was like a computer. I figured it out in my head. The first couple of days I was shaky, I didn't know whether I was on the right track. But the first day we did a hundred dollars, and when it kept on going up and up and up, I figured I was on to something. It almost became anticlimactic. Now it's a game: How many stores can I open? Can I open a thousand? Two thousand? Can I get the store I want in Paris? What kind of deal can I make with the Japanese? It wasn't as much fun as the old days of Saucier, running around trying to convince Midwestern housewives to make butter-bound bordelaise sauce.

John Diebold, MANAGEMENT CONSULTANT

Effecting Change, Leaving an Impression

I've always been interested in ideas and in trying to get ideas across. My own measure of success has been: When I'm very old, will I have had some impact on the time I lived in? I think that with ideas, the way you have to do that is through institutions. At least that's the route I chose. I think that if you influence the ideas and the direction of an enterprise employing a couple hundred thousand people, you have a multiplier impact. Whether those are changes in the way universities go about things or the way businesses go about things, both have a considerable impact; human beings work in jobs, and these are a large part of their lives.

An Interest in Problems

I'm less interested in sitting with solutions. I'm more interested in problems and in trying to move ahead with ideas and things. I chose not to try to build a company that would do routine stuff. We're really trying to deal with cutting-edge problems for government and business and educational institutions all around the world. I could have gone in the direction, for example, of programming computers. I don't find that interesting. I'd rather work on policy problems. The business is totally a function of what I think is interesting to do. There are a lot of ways we could have gone that probably would have been better financially, like making pencils, or doing an electronic equivalent to that. Those are things people should do, but that isn't what I should do.

The Main Measure of Success

That these are the things I want to do is the main measure of success. I think you can measure this sort of thing in a lot of different ways, and I test those against my own: Are you having any kind of impact on modern, major organizations, through getting changes made and things done? I think we are, and that's what I set out to do.

Periodically people ask, "What would you do differently?" Well, sure, a hundred things I'd do differently that day, but basically I'm doing the same thing I've always done and I'm very happy with it.

John DePasquale, DIRECT MARKETING

But Is It Worth It?

Would I do it over again? Absolutely. Would I recommend that other people do it? Absolutely. But only if you're cut out for it. Because really, the costs of becoming successful are excessive. Unless you are ready to shoulder these excessive costs, don't go into the kitchen because you're going to find it hot.

You have to be willing to give up a lot. There are pots at the end of the rainbow, whenever and wherever that is. If you are successful there are some nice perks that come your way, but you certainly have to be willing to give up a lot.

There are times in the day, well, for everybody, but certainly for the entrepreneur, when it seems so overwhelming you're not exactly sure whether it's worth it. For many it isn't. Whatever the amount of hours you think you have to spend, triple it. I was working eighteen to twenty hours a day two years in a row. I wasn't loving it, and I was paying a lot of prices, both those I knew about then and those I didn't.

Christopher Whittle, CHAIRMAN, *ESQUIRE* MAGAZINE

Career vs. Life

I don't think career success and personal success are completely disconnected. There are some pretty significant strings between the two, but they don't perfectly coincide. They also conflict sometimes; they can definitely get in each other's way.

I always look at success from two perspectives—according to my own standards and then according to the world's standards. And according to the world's standards, yes, I view myself as a success. Not hugely. By the world's standards, yes, if you at age thirty-four or thirty-five have a fifty-million-dollar publishing enterprise, built from scratch, you're successful. I have a whole other group of measures, and by my measures, I view myself as moderately successful.

A Balanced Existence

One measure of personal success is balance, and by that I mean a balanced existence, that your life is more

than just your career. Mine is definitely not balanced.
Right now mine is predominantly my career. And therefore, I haven't been successful in that regard because it
consumes disproportionate amounts of my energy and
time. It's clear that some part of me wants it that way.

Fame and Fortune

There's a line in a song in *Evita,* something like "Fortune and fame are not what they promised to be." That's
yet to be answered. Let's put it this way: It does not
appear to be automatic. It doesn't appear that if you one
day have some degree of fortune and some degree of
fame—I don't view myself as famous or wealthy—the
benefits flow naturally from there. I think that you can
take those things and apply them in certain ways and get
benefits, but I don't think that one day you achieve fortune and "Ah ha! Isn't this wonderful?" I don't think it
works that way. You have to channel them into something else. I'm on fragile ground here because I would
be hypocritical to deny that fortune and fame are not a
motivating factor. But I'm being honest in saying that
they are not really what I'm looking for. They're kind
of things along the way.

Richard Leibner, AGENT

The Greatest Thing

I have the greatest thing in the whole world: freedom.
I have my own business. If I were going to become anybody at a big talent agency, I'd have to spend a lot of
time going to the coast, and then you're not home
watching your kids grow up. You have to figure out how
to enjoy what you have and not kill yourself and how to
maintain your integrity and how to keep a quality level.
You've got to be a little nuts to play these games for the
sake of trading your name in for their name.

I'm not shooting to be a multimillionaire: To me that's

bullshit. There's a perfect balance in my life. I know I'll be secure in older age. I'm basically happy. I want to get out before I'm too old to have fun, and I hope that the most loyal people will carry on, or the kids. I'm wrapped up in having fun, helping other people. I'm making more money now than I ever thought I'd make.

David Liederman, DAVID'S COOKIES

I Want to Get Rich

I work seven days a week. And you know, what's the point? You really have to think about that: What's the point? People who were not born with money and then begin to make money don't know what to do with it. All they know how to do is make more of it. I see stories about people who had money when they were growing up, and they have all these nice things and they go to nice places. I have nice houses, but I'm never in them because I'm always in this hole of an office down here. Somehow the quality of life isn't that good and you don't know where to get off. When do you get off? That's a good question. I don't know. I can't answer that.

All I thought about when I was growing up was, I want to get rich. That's all I thought about, and I was always interested in food so I put the two together. So now I'm rich. But to what end? That's the problem. A lot of people try to buy David's Cookies, a lot of big companies. At this point I wouldn't even think of selling David's Cookies because I haven't made the statement yet. The only ego thing I have involved in David's Cookies is that I want to have the largest specialty-cookie company in the United States.

Wally Amos, FOUNDER, FAMOUS AMOS COOKIES

To Be in Control

I just wanted to make a living. I'd been in show business for fourteen years, and I didn't want to deal with show business anymore. I just wanted to be in control of my life. I had lost all my hopes of being wealthy, of being an important person. I used to want to be an important manager, I used to want to make a lot of money—but that changed, and I just wanted to make a living.

I knew that Famous Amos would give me a steady income. In show business you don't have steady income; some weeks you do, and some weeks you don't.

I knew I was going to make it before I started, because the level I was trying to make it on was very obtainable. I just wanted to make a living. I figured that there were over twelve million people in the Los Angeles area, and I should be able to get a hundred a day who would buy my cookies. At the time the cookies were three dollars a pound, so I said, "Hey, if I make three-hundred dollars a day, that'll pay all my expenses and be enough left over for me to pay my bills and have a little money, and I'll be doing what I want to do."

I'm just a big kid, a silly kid. I just want it to be fun. And I'm having fun. When I started doing this, the one thing I decided was, I was going to do it to please me. When it's not fun, I'll quit.

Jan Stuart, SKIN-CARE PRODUCTS FOR MEN

Goals

I just knew I wanted to leave my mark. I wanted to do something. My big ambition has always been to make money, not to the point of going out there and trying to hustle the dollars and be called a wheeler-dealer, but to be called a legitimate businessman.

Being a financial success isn't my ultimate goal. I could have become financially successful two or three years ago in what I wanted to do. I don't want to sell my soul like a lot of other business people do. I've got a good quality product, and people are telling me now, "Well, Jan, if you came out with a product that wasn't as good, you'd make more profit, you could make a lot more money." But I knew in the long run I would put my name up, so I came up with a real quality product.

Jeffrey Feinman, PROMOTIONAL CONSULTANT

Insurance

I personally only want to do stuff that is fun for me. If tomorrow I could make half a million dollars a year selling life insurance, I wouldn't do it because I can't imagine anything worse than meeting people and telling them you're a life-insurance salesman.

David Brown, FILM PRODUCER

When the pain outweighs the pleasure, I'll give it up. That's always been my rule. When I didn't have a sou to my name, I always had a pact with my wife—all three of them—that if things were too tough I could quit my job, find something else. That still goes.

Hal David, SONGWRITER

There's Nothing More Fun Than Success

It was important for me to earn a living. It was important for me to stand on my own two feet yesterday, not tomorrow. My goal was to achieve a good life doing something that I liked to do right.

Defining success is hard. I guess success is feeling good about yourself while you're doing what you like to do. Real success, the one that lasts, is a slow development, an accumulation of experience.

Look, there's nothing more fun than to succeed, no matter what you do. What success can do to some people can be devastating. I've seen terrible examples of that, but I'm not talking about that. There's just such a nice feeling deep inside when you succeed, that you did it. You may not have done it alone, but you're reassured that you're really there, and you really have contributed something. Success is good.

One of the lucky things is I've had so much fun with my work. I'm a hard-working person, but there's nothing in the world like turning on the radio in the car and hearing your song. I love to write. Writing is always hard: I forget how hard it is until I'm doing it. You just remember how nice it is.

I love my life. I have had a lucky life. My work has been successful and recognized, so I've had great artistic satisfaction. I've had great financial satisfaction.

David Brown, FILM PRODUCER

Master Plans

I find that in my particular world goals are fictional, because you put yourself in the way of opportunities. You have something in the mail all the time, an idea. I've never understood people who have five-year goals or ten-year goals or anything like that. Most of my opportunities have come out of left field, including motion pictures. But, I was always working at something related to it. As far as a goal, did I want to be president of a motion-picture company or editor of *Time*? I never had specific goals like that. I wanted to get on in the world and find out what there was out there that might be interesting to do, rather than having a very specific goal.

I wanted to put myself in the way of luck and success and say, "Here's where I am, I'm a working person." But I didn't have a master plan.

Jerry Rubin, BUSINESS NETWORKING SALONS

What happens to you is usually better than whatever your goals are. I think it's always important to keep your mind on your goal, but also be aware that life will present you the real results.

You set a goal for yourself, then something else happens. You go to the theater one night and in the third row you see someone you haven't seen for a while, and that reminds you to call that person and that changes your life. Well, you didn't go that night to meet that person, that was the farthest thing from your mind, but it happened. And the play was awful. However, that was the accident, so maybe what I'm doing here is also. I have an idea what my goal is, but maybe tomorrow I'll meet someone who'll add a little twist to this.

Christopher Whittle, CHAIRMAN, *ESQUIRE* MAGAZINE

Success teaches me. It has definitely forged me. If I look back on the last thirteen years, I am a different person than I was. It has developed my character in many ways, because it's been so hard. It forces a self-scrutiny and a toughness on self and self-criticism that I think is very healthy. The acceptance of responsibility really does those things.

Character Building

My partner, Phillip Moffitt, said years ago, and I agree with him, that entrepreneuring is a character-building experience. I don't think there's any question. If you start with reasonably good raw material, it turns into a pretty good finished product.

I believe in beginning luck. I believe that we got programmed in certain things early on that we didn't have anything to do with. That was luck. I think that *happened*. And you're always playing off that beginning luck. But after that, I don't believe in it much, and part of that comes from my own experience. I don't think we've had a lot of luck, meaning that one day I went, "Wow! Where did that come from?" Most things have been very direct results. I wouldn't generalize that: It's a strictly personal experience. I often wonder if it's true elsewhere.

Jerry Rubin, BUSINESS NETWORKING SALONS

Changing Dreams and Realities

My transition from revolutionary to networking was just a gradual readjustment-to-reality process in that I discovered that political labels didn't necessarily make happy individuals. Also, I realized that money is a way to keep score. It isn't necessarily all bad. Every society has some way of keeping score. We have money.

There are some obvious differences in the way I think now. I used to believe that if somebody was poor, they were better than somebody who was wealthy. That was distorted. I had a lot of distorted views; I had a lot of good views, too. I'm not putting myself down. It was part of a dream that the disinherited would inherit the earth—and abolish inheritance. But that was a dream and you can't impose a dream on reality.

Reality chips away at your dream. I'm still alive. I'm not the dream, I'm me. That's also important, always to separate yourself from anything you do. I'm different from the dream of Networking. I think it was important for me to say to myself, "I am not the image of that person that people say was Jerry Rubin at the end of the sixties." See, if I hadn't done that I'd be dead, because then I would have been living other people's lives. I created an image. I did it, but once the image was created, other people kept re-creating it for their own needs, which took my autonomy away.

I thought of myself as a success in the sixties. I'd have to be extremely neurotic not to. In terms of nationwide movements, an internationally known trial, challenging the Pentagon, a couple of people turning on an idea that swept the country. You set goals for yourself, but then you achieve other things that are just as good, but you never could have imagined them because the categories did not exist. I think that's called serendipity. Only a real pessimist would put his hands on his head and say, "I failed because one goal wasn't achieved." Look at the big picutre, for God's sake.

John DePasquale, DIRECT MARKETING

What was my own thing? I didn't have the foggiest idea. But I knew I wanted to do it.

III. THE SUCCESS MOTIVE

Why some people want—and need—success more than others: motives, influences, and conditions for success

There's no consensus, only speculation, on the sources of success. Theories are proposed that it comes from hardship or security, deprivation or encouragement, fear or confidence. The following are some thoughts successful people have on motivations that might have influenced their own success.

THE SUCCESSFUL CHILDHOOD

Milton Glaser, GRAPHIC DESIGNER

Support vs. Resistance

People always ask what accounts for success. In terms of supportive issues, my mother was sort of the model for the supporting mother. She really said all my life, "You can do it, you're the best," all the right things. My father was appropriately resistant. He said, "Show me. I don't believe it."

It became sort of a metaphor for the world. I always felt I could overcome my father's resistance because I had the support of my mother, and I suspect that that persists. I always feel I can overcome the world, or the world's standards, or criticism, or whatever, because I had my mother's assurance behind me. That combination, resistance and support, gives people a little extra advantage.

Jerry Rubin, BUSINESS NETWORKING SALONS

Happy Children Are Handicapped

I was an unsuccessful child. Being an unsuccessful child helps you be more successful later. I think happy children are handicapped because they don't have that edge. If you're overdeprived, then you get paralysis and neurosis, extreme forms of sickness, unfortunately. It's just that right amount of deprivation, where you're treated very well but then deprived. For example, I inherited a kind of feeling that I could conquer the world, but then I was also mistreated and deprived. So that right combination together produced ambition, the ability to think in global terms.

I don't know where I got that, really, because I just grew up in Cincinnati, Ohio. My father was a bread-truck driver and then a teamster official: I didn't get it from him, really. Maybe I got it from baseball: How would I get it from baseball? Some attitudes you just pick up.

I always thought I was special but that I was deprived, so that was perfect. I've never doubted that I would be successful, for some reason. I'm not speaking necessarily of economically deprived. The deprivation that I got was growing up in a very opinionated, uninspiring situation. That's my deprivation. But I had a kind of superior feeling.

David Brown, FILM PRODUCER

Compensation for Deprivation

I think success has to do with your parents, and the kind of role models they were. I think it has to do with fear and insecurity. I had an insecure childhood, the product of divorced parents. I think it has to do with whether you're popular at school or not. I was not.

I was always a loner, and I think people who are loners tend to get their satisfaction in work. I remember so well when my office was on the top floor of 37 West Fifty-seventh Street, when I was editor-in-chief of *Liberty Magazine,* and on long holidays I would be miserable. I'd walk around saying, "Why isn't anyone here?" I was a mess. I had other interests but I was not popular—I had no, and probably to this day have no, resources. I was not a prepossessing athletic man-of-the-year, star-of-the-class kind of person. So, a certain amount of deprivation—while I don't recommend it for children—seems to run through a lot of success stories. You tend to compensate in your work life for the love and admiration and recognition you didn't get in your adolescent life.

Work is rewarding. It isn't that it's keeping you busy, but it's satisfying you. It becomes your lover. Your office, your place of work, is a place where you are somebody, and where you can achieve something. It's a very personal thing. I've always felt that the work life was reliable. Lovers could abandon you, other things could fail, but work was always there if you took care of it. Work was a relationship that generally gave back what you put into it, if you were sincere. As early as my first job I realized this.

I'm not psychoanalyzing myself, but I was very shy and the world of adolescence is a world of physical achievement, good looks, popularity. I can remember being rejected for a baseball team when I was perhaps eight years old, and it stays in my mind. You remember those things fifty, sixty years into your life. I wanted some achievement; that was my unconscious as well as conscious desire. I wanted to become famous. I wasn't interested in money; that never entered my mind. It was a very happy means rather than an end.

There are very many successful people who have come out of terrific families. I don't think there's any substitute for a supportive family. I don't think that what I've experienced, and what others have experienced, is a necessary concomitant of success. It's one way.

I think everyone's success is indigenous to his or her own personality and background. Who's to say that my kind of success is as good as the kind of success I might have achieved if I had not felt as deprived as I did? Success in the broad sense is learning to live with yourself and getting a certain degree of joy out of your life span. I can't advise happy people. I don't know enough about them.

Hal David, SONGWRITER

Success Comes from Need

I have two sons, and they've told me they always knew that their mother and I were there, and that gave them a sense of confidence. My father was an invalid, so it wasn't the same. That helped me. It may have taken away some aspects of my life, but it gave me others.

Jan Stuart, SKIN-CARE PRODUCTS FOR MEN

I always had visions of somebody saying, "Jan, you're great, you're terrific, we want to put you into business." That doesn't happen at all. You have to prove yourself.

I believe to this day that I was fortunate not to find anybody to help me out, because I was one of those people who had to do it himself. I don't think I would have been happy if somebody had given it to me on a silver platter. I think that it was my fortune to go out and start something from scratch and learn for myself what was going to make me happy and what I had to do.

Christopher Whittle, CHAIRMAN, *ESQUIRE* MAGAZINE

Motivations

There is definitely a fear, I think, in the achievement of success, and it goes through different stages. There's one stage of it that's the fear of never getting there at all, which is generally earlier in your career. And then once you have success, there's the fear of maintenance, which is a different kind of fear. Can you go forward? Will you go backward? And they produce the same result, which is that you work hard. And they also produce a form of acceleration. There's a saying that if you aren't growing, you're dying. Businesses cannot be static; they must be going up or going down—they never stop flat. I don't know where that came from, but I think it's right. You're constantly pushing for more because you feel if you don't do that, it will go the other way. That motivation is definitely there.

I think a lot of that early fear of never achieving success comes from various personal insecurities that exist early on. A lot of people will tell you that most great successes were due to great insecurities. You work out of your insecurities a lot. I've worked out of mine.

You may start out with these certain insecurities that drive you toward being successful, and what begins to happen is that you begin to amass positive evidence that counterbalances the insecurities. All of a sudden you realize that you can do things, and you have real confidence levels. If you've done enough things well and you see that you can do them, at some point you go, "I can do these things." You know that you have it in you to be able to do this or that, so you don't stop. You know you can weather it, you can get through.

Edward McCabe, ADVERTISING EXECUTIVE

Trying Harder

I've very definitely made trade-offs because of my business, but it isn't cause and effect, it's a personal thing. It has to do with the fact that, not having an education, I always felt handicapped. Therefore, I felt I had to throw myself into it more deeply than any of my competition. I had to try harder, work harder, devote myself 140 percent to it, and as a result I was blind to everything else I was doing in my life and made a lot of mistakes. I wouldn't say it has necessarily to do with success. It has to do with sucess in *my* instance, where I blotted out everything else. I didn't have time for anything else because I was afraid that if I didn't devote everything to work they'd catch me and send me back to high school.

My father died when I was very young, and I felt when I was eight years old that I was the man of the house and that I was in charge. By the time I was nine or ten I had seven or eight newspaper routes, worked Sundays at a newsstand, had all kinds of jobs, did all kinds of things, and had frustrations over the way my mother was handling my father's estate. I just wasn't quite wise enough—or old enough—to get anybody's attention, but I felt that it was all up to me, which probably started it.

Success Comes from a Sense of Necessity

It's abject failure: no food, no home. That became the instinct, the overriding instinct. Sure, I have people who say, "This isn't a life-or-death situation." I don't want to hear that. It could be the littlest thing. No toilet paper in the men's room? I go berserk. The day the no-smoking-in-elevators law was passed I went up and down this agency screaming, "Why aren't there ashtrays in every foyer by the elevators?" You can't force people not to smoke in the elevators, and then not have ashtrays. I get crazy over little things. In my personal life, too, unfortunately. There's an unfortunate consistency to this trait; it works very well in business and doesn't work too well in life.

David Brown, FILM PRODUCER

Self-Faith

I think to be successful you must think successful at an early age. That requires a certain degree of naïvete. You may be one person among a thousand desks, but you're the one who's not awed or intimidated by people in authority and that's very important. I've always felt that if I had an office and a pad of paper, I would think of something, and that's always been true. I've always been entrepreneurial, even as an employee. I never felt like I was one of the boys, as we used to say. It gave me trouble when I joined the American Newspaper Guild because I'd look around at all the gray heads and I'd say, "By God, they're all united against the bosses, but I'm not one of these guys—I'm one of the other people! There's an impossible gulf between us."

Hal David, SONGWRITER

A Balance of Faith and Doubt

I always had two feelings. I don't anymore, but there was a time in my life I was schizophrenic in the sense that half of me knew I was terrific and the other half of me said no. I wondered. But part of me always felt I could do it.

I loved writing; I loved hearing my songs, and I really thought deep down I was good, but I was frightened as hell. What was I going to do if I didn't succeed? I didn't have an answer. I knew how to write something, put some words together. That was really all I knew. My father ran a delicatessen. I didn't want to do that. I didn't have a business background. I wasn't a professional; I wasn't a lawyer or a doctor. I was frightened out of my skin.

Richard Leibner, AGENT

Pessimism

I am a pessimist by nature. In the beginning days, before I reached that point of earning, that point of confidence in what I could do, I always motivated myself by the feeling that I would fail. I always drove myself by pessimism.

I used to drive myself, dream about it at night, and have myself in such a pitch before I ever went into the room to do a deal that I pushed myself to the optimum. That's not as necessary anymore. The people I was negotiating with didn't know how I felt; with them I was strong.

Milton Glaser, GRAPHIC DESIGNER

Motive for Success: Revenge

I have always felt that the big motivation for sucess is revenge, revenge against the world, against anyone who humiliated you, against your sister, brother, mother, father, cousin—any and all of them. Early embarrassments, all that kind of thing. "I'll show them." I don't think you get rid of that, those embedded issues in your life. They may not have the same driving force as they once did, or you may reach a point where you say, "OK, there it is. I proved it, I was right and you were wrong," and so the imperative for maintaining it may not be as strong.

In people I know who are very driven toward success, it seems that either self-justification or revenge keeps the furnace going.

THE MAN (OR WOMAN) AND HIS BUSINESS

Lois Wyse, ADVERTISING EXECUTIVE

Self-employment: It Doesn't Matter

I didn't care about working for myself.

Working hard and taking responsibility doesn't mean you have to be in business for yourself: A lot of people who run major corporations aren't in business for themselves. They make a lot more money than I do and they make much bigger decisions, but they're not in business for themselves.

I don't know that there are enormous advantages to being in business for yourself. I don't think that's terribly important. I think what's important is to have a certain amount of freedom, which you can have whether you're in business for yourself or not.

Jeffrey Feinman, PROMOTIONAL CONSULTANT

Self-employment: It Does Matter

I had gone from clerk to vice-president in a large marketing firm. I was twenty-eight years old and there was nowhere left to go. I said, "If there is ever going to be a time when I have more energy and less to lose—when I can always go out and make a living—it is now."

The company was about one hundred people: I was number-two guy. I could go no further. The guy who owned it showed no evidence that he was going to retire. The guy I replaced there as executive vice-president was an older guy who'd had a fight with the owner one day and was fired, and I said, "That's me. I'll be forty-six years old and have a fight with the owner and be out."

At the same time, a friend called me at work one night

at 11:30 and said, "I don't know much about business, but it seems rather bizarre to me that at 11:30 at night you're there working for this guy. It seems to me all you're doing is building his business so his kids can be richer. Why aren't you doing that for you?" That's exactly what I was doing. So I left.

George Lang, RESTAURATEUR

Variety

I thrive on variety. Even in food. If I have my druthers, I have not just a main course, which you start and end with and the only relief you get is the couple of vegetables, but I prefer a variety of relishes and condiments and chutneys and so forth. I like a variety of tastes to relieve the monotony of a single flavor.

To give you a sense of the variety, look at what is on my desk right now: a project in Florida, a three-thousand-unit luxury condominium; the Thanksgiving menu for Café des Artistes; an article I just wrote, which I now have to edit; plans for a party I am giving for Plácido Domingo and Eva Marton in my home, for which I must cook; a letter from a former secretary asking me to help her with ways of teaching handicapped children about foods; a company that is asking me to design a new take-apart-put-together wine cellar that will fit in a professional kitchen; a Carnegie Hall matter where I am a board member and we are working on several things; questions from a hotel chain in the West, for which I am a consultant in planning their Austin hotel; plans for a restaurant I designed in Kansas City.

I'll tell you something that will turn off everybody who reads this: I just have a little more brains and more energy. I sleep only three or four hours.

IV. CREATIVE FORCES

The creative and innovative elements in success: how they work, how they are maintained, why they are crucial

Good ideas—never mind great ones—don't grow on trees. For the most part, the best ideas develop slowly and need careful nurturing. The twin abilities of being able to spot and elaborate on a good idea are not only common to, but are vital to, the successful entrepreneur. Furthermore, one good idea simply isn't enough; a regular supply is required for sustained success.

The discussion that follows deals with ideas—creation and innovation—how they are encouraged, managed, and kept fresh.

David Brown, FILM PRODUCER

Naïveté

I did a television show with Bob Guccione, the publisher of *Penthouse,* and David Susskind some years ago on the mythology of success. Bob and I both agreed that success requires a certain degree of naïvete, impracticality—as in Bob thinking he could overcome *Playboy* from an attic in London.

When Richard Zanuck and I bought *Jaws,* if we had read it twice we'd have known it was an impossible movie to make. It required naïvete, omniscience, a suspension of expertise. The same thing when my wife and I put together a magazine called *Femme,* which became the present-day *Cosmopolitan.* Who was looking for a magazine? We did it on the kitchen table.

I do believe, at least for my kind of success, had I been a more sensible, rational person, with more experience in some of these fields, I never would have succeeded as I have. People say, "Were you frightened of becoming editor of a national magazine at an early age, or taking over these jobs?" I should have been. But I had this dumb feeling that somehow I could do it—which wasn't cockiness, but a kind of naïvete or innocence.

Norma Kamali, FASHION DESIGNER

The Virtues of Ignorance

In the beginning, I was too stupid to know about the risks, and I had a lot of enthusiasm. I am so grateful that I *didn't* know; I got through the beginning on the strength of ignorance and lots of enthusiasm. If I had known then what I know now, I don't know if I would have begun. I *think* I would have, because so much of it was the desire in me.

When people tell me I can't do something, it only brings up from my gut this response of "Oh, *really?* Well, I'll show you," and I want to do it. I have this stubborn streak in me that if I want to do it, I'm going to do it.

What's changed is my desires. I don't know what they will be five or ten years from now, but I do know that keeping the goals interesting and different is very important to me, so that I'm always dealing with the ignorance of what I'm getting into. And a lot of enthusiasm.

Wally "Famous" Amos

No Answers

I was very much undercapitalized because I didn't know. I just went, "Telephone's going to be so much, rent's going to be so much, salaries are going to be so much, and I need so much for food costs." I used common sense, I thought. I think that, in my naïvete, I was able to do it because if I had had all the training, and been an expert, I would have told myself, "You can't do this, can't do this, can't do this." So I think it's important, really, not to know. It can be done.

Ignorance can be helpful. You talk yourself out of things when you think you have the answers. We never have the answers, we just *think* we have the answers.

It was trial and error, and there were adjustments. I think what people have to understand is that there's not a blueprint that says, "Here's the way it is," and you do this first, this second, and this third—it doesn't happen like that. Life doesn't happen like that, and business is just an extension of life. So you have to know that there are going to be detours, there are going to be obstacles. But there are always answers to whatever challenges come into your life. You know that and you just deal with them.

Christopher Whittle, CHAIRMAN, *ESQUIRE* MAGAZINE

"We Didn't Understand the Extent of What We Were Getting Into"

I can think of two times in my career when my partner, Phillip Moffitt, and I had been told by lots of different parties, "This can't work," and "You can't pull this off." But I don't think that's *why* we pulled them off. I don't think that's why we started them at all. I don't think we understood the extent of what we were getting into. We weren't told "you can't do it" until after we began.

Esquire is a perfect example. *Esquire,* I think, will go down as one of the biggest publishing turnarounds ever, because the losses were astronomical. I do want to qualify something. *Esquire,* for the record, was bad off financially; it was not bad off as an editorial product. We just didn't quite understand how bad the situation was financially. I mean, it was finished. It was in dire financial straits, and when we got in we realized that it was bad. Everyone then was telling us, "This is going to be incredibly difficult to do, if it's at all possible."

I think that negativism fuels your desire, but it was not a motivating factor. We didn't say, "Hey, let's go do that to prove to the people that are telling us that we can't." We went and did things because they were challenges.

If we had known how badly off it was, I don't think we would have taken it on, because we would have thought we couldn't muster the resources, we just weren't in a position at that time. If we had said to ourselves before we started, "We're going to have to go off and do this," I don't think we could have done it, because I think the evidence against us would have been so overwhelming.

There's a phrase, *robust naïvete,* which I've heard a few times and which I think is appropriately applied to entrepreneurs. It's this kind of major innocence.

David Brown, FILM PRODUCER

Sense of Wonder

I feel success is compounded of a certain amount of innocence and naïvete. I've often wondered why I don't use certain writers and certain people who have grown older, who are my age. Because I think they've had it, they're gone. Why aren't they good anymore? They were so successful twenty years ago, ten years ago, thrity years ago. They're still healthy, but they've lost something. I think that they lose their enthusiasm and innocence and their awe of the world, and that's a youthful quality.

When you've seen it all and you've done it all and when

every problem reminds you of a problem you've faced before, it's very tough to have that bright-eyed, bushy-tailed feeling, particularly in this city of New York.

I still feel in the morning that anything could happen in New York. And it does.

Jerry Rubin, BUSINESS NETWORKING SALONS

Gee Whiz

I think the fact I'm from Ohio is very good because it gives me a kind of "gee whiz" attitude toward life. I'm curious. Curiosity is the most important thing. You have to always be curious and ask questions. I see people who come on like they know it all. I don't understand that. In my mind, I still live in Cincinnati. I'm physically in Manhattan, but mentally I'm in Cincinnati.

There have been times when I've been so depressed that it was hard to be curious about anything. But usually I'm pretty lucky. I've heard this elsewhere—it's not an original thought—that people born in the Midwest have an advantage over people born in the East or in California because there's kind of an American faith in people, kind of an American naïvete that lives in the Midwest.

Now of course I know a lot of people in Cincinnati who were eighty years old when they were fifteen years old; they never lived, they just died as teenagers, and it's sad to watch. So obviously we're talking here about potentials and possibilities. But I remember I was talking to a friend once, and we realized he was from Columbus, Ohio, and I was from Cincinnati, and we realized that's part of why we were friends. Because we both had kind of a sense of wonder about Vietnam, New York, the world, people, and so forth, and we weren't cynical. I'm not really cynical; I can put on a cynical attitude like anybody, and I might be cynical at moments, but my general attitude has never been cynical.

Jeffrey Hollender, NETWORK FOR LEARNING

Finding New Problems

Generally speaking, when I'm doing something that I've done before and I'm burned out, I figure it's time to teach someone else how to do it. The teaching of the project to someone else makes it interesting again, because trying to show someone how to do it once you've figured out how is a whole different problem.

If I woke up in the morning and I didn't want to come to work, I probably wouldn't. I wake up some mornings and I think, "I don't know how I'm going to do this," or "I don't want to do this," but I never wake up feeling bored. Partially, I've been more fortunate than most people because my business has changed so rapidly and so quickly. As the business changes, you get to do new things you couldn't do before. You have opportunities to constantly hire new people. So I haven't had to try to keep myself interested.

Dr. Richard Winter, EXECUTIVE HEALTH EXAMINERS

Something Interesting

I didn't look at it as entering business or making money; I looked at it as something that would be more interesting to do in terms of getting out. The problem with adult medical practice, for me, was most of it was boring as hell. I think that's basically true of all doctors. Some realize it and hate it, and others don't realize it and don't know why they yell at their wives.

The problem is that 98 percent or more of what you see is what we call garbage. I'm talking the way doctors talk to each other. The guys will be sitting at lunch at the hospital, and ask what kind of day you had. "Eh, all garbage." Like that. Now, patients don't like to hear that; how can a doctor speak that way about a human being?

But if you see enough of that all day long, which you have to to make a living, well what's interesting about it? And that's basically your day. So what I used to do was sit around hoping someone would have a nice heart attack so I could do something interesting. It sounds terrible, but from a purely professional standpoint that was a challenge.

David Brown, FILM PRODUCER

Having Done It All

We've done it all. Between my partner, Richard Zanuck, and me, we've had thirty-five years of executive experience, twenty for me and fifteen for him. Like political office, there's a life span to that sort of thing. You don't want to do it anymore. And the reason you don't want to do it is that you lose your innocence, you lose your enthusiasm.

When you've used up your bag of tricks, you might want to move on. Everybody has a repertory of some sort in life. Fortunately, motion-picture production enables you to move new groups, younger people. When you make movies, every one is a separate enterprise, with a separate cast, a separate group, a separate crew, usually. But when you're an executive, the first day you say, "Oh, my God, we're faced with *this* again."

There's a life span for certain types of authority—unless you're a founder. My wife has been editor of *Cosmopolitan* for over seventeen years, and she's as sprightly as the day she was born, but she has a particular passion for it. It's her child. Harold Ross had it for *The New Yorker*. But magazines have a new script every week or every month.

Even the founders of great corporations are generally superseded by professional managers who not infrequently surpass the achievements of the founder. They couldn't have created the business, but the business could never have reached the heights it did without the professional managers who took it along.

I left New American Library when I was asked to come back to Hollywood, when my team, the Zanucks, regained their power at Twentieth Century-Fox. I was ready to leave publishing at that point because, although I was successful at it, I really found movies more fun. At that time, too, I still had my innocence.

I can't think of anything I would have done differently. I never turned down the editorship of *The New Yorker*, which I would have loved to have. I would cheerfully have left the motion picture business for that.

Much as I favor a nongeriatric approach to life, I don't think I could do *The New Yorker* now. I do think those jobs are best undertaken earlier in life, not only because of innocence but there's a danger as you grow older of not having quite the fresh ideas you had before, because you've OD'd on ideas all your life. At twenty-five I could have gone into any magazine—and did—and thrown out ideas for departments and done this, that, and the other thing. Now I think I would remember departments I did in the past. There's a law of diminishing returns.

I think what I can best do now for the rest of my life is something I've never done before. Maybe produce a Broadway play, or something in television. I would be fresh for that, because I haven't done it. But to go into something I've already done—magazine editing, publishing, being a movie executive, as myself and my partner have been offered many times—would be déjà vu time. It's very rare that someone in a position for thirty years can overcome the disadvantage of overexposure and overexperience.

Milton Glaser, GRAPHIC DESIGNER

Jeopardy and Caution

New York magazine was very embarrassing because it was ugly, badly put together technically. Once you start doing something, you're on a treadmill and it's very hard to chart a course. It took about a year and a half to understand what the hell the fault could be. It wasn't the low point of my career by any means. It was the most embarrassing, the most humiliating, but not the low point. There is this liveliness that comes out of difficulty and now knowing whether you're going to succeed or fail— a sense of risk or jeopardy. I must have liked something about it.

In the case of *New York* magazine, we were lucky enough to make it work. It probably would have been a low point if we'd failed. If I couldn't turn it around, if I couldn't figure it out, if the magazine had died, then it probably would have been a blow of significant dimensions. I think the professional low point was when Clay Felker and I tried to do *Esquire* afterward, which I shouldn't have done. I think I was at that time used up in the magazine business. I'd done too much of it, designed too many of them. I knew too much and that made me cautious.

INNOVATION

Edward McCabe, ADVERTISING EXECUTIVE

What **Hasn't** *Been Done*

The essence of innovative thinking is to go and do what hasn't been done. The reason what hasn't been done hasn't been done is that most people don't think they can do it. I think you generate innovation by refusing to accept things the way they are. That doesn't mean you necessarily want to create new things: You find a way to create them out of being impatient with the way things are. On the other hand, there are people who really can see ways to create new things.

It's not necessarily an impatience with what is. They just have a vision. Some people come along who just have an idea and they can see it very clearly.

One of my nagging doubts about the Perdue chicken campaign was that it wasn't new. When I was first working on it, I had this nagging feeling that it wasn't good enough. It was good on a lot of levels, but there have been other campaigns with company spokesmen.

In advertising, there is no tried and true because the fodder for the creative man is the fact that he should not be doing anything tried and true. So I like to see something that I've never seen before, that's totally unique. That's very hard to do. It always comes out of something else.

Milton Glaser, GRAPHIC DESIGNER

Professionalism

Professionalism is not only a conspiracy against the public, as it was once described, but it's really the enemy of invention in the sense that, by definition, professionalism means diminished risk. You go to a professional because you don't want to take any chances, because the performance level is guaranteed, and the performance level gets to be guaranteed when you do the same thing over and over again, basically without changing it. Once you become professional, and reduce risk, you also inevitably reduce the imagination and the possibility for innovation. Everybody always wants to be a professional, to get to the point where they are considered professional. Once you've arrived, however, you find that it's enormously difficult to maintain the position of being innovative, risk-taking, idiosyncratic—and you need those things. You have to keep that an element in your work.

The fundamental question of professional life is: How do people manage to survive *and* keep themselves alive to their work by not repeating their own history and not capitalizing on their success with increasingly weakened responses? I think that's everybody's problem. I don't know how to do it. I basically change what I do, the nature of what I do. I started out more or less as a kind of comic illustrator when I was very young, and then I moved to illustration in general. Then I became interested in design and went into the book jacket-design business, and I started doing more things like posters. We started to do a large range of corporate work and trademarks and stuff, and then went into the magazine business at the same time. In recent years I've been doing more interior design—supermarkets and food-related projects, packaging. And now I'm back into the magazine business, on a kind of consulting basis.

Deadlines aren't destructive at all. Constraints are not destructive. What is destructive is the sense that you have to repeat precisely what you've done, and that you have to deliver a guaranteed product every time. Clients ask all the time that I repeat what I've done; basically your reputation is always based on what you've done, and my interest has always been in avoiding that.

I try to allow the work to go where it will, but that's usually against professional criteria. In professional work, you're supposed to know what you're doing before you start. You make your decisions because you want to diminish risk in professional work, so you generally solve it and then do it, and what you don't get is the vital, stumbling amateurishness that you want in your work. That's true of a lot of things, of more things than one would categorize as art. It's true of any invention of any insight or any kind.

George Lang, RESTAURATEUR

Routine

I not only don't want to imitate anybody, but I sure as hell don't want to imitate myself, either. The minute I begin to repeat myself, I will probably become a ticket taker at a public swimming pool. I don't know; I would probably have considerably more time to contemplate various parts of my body.

Many fine professionals stopped growing at a certain point because routine got them.

Hal David, SONGWRITER

Risk Taking

I don't think it becomes *harder* to take risks as you become more successful; I think it becomes less wise. Let me put it this way. You take a million dollars and you put it in the bank at 10 percent interest, and you sit there that year and make $100,000. By the time you have the million dollars and it's earning the $100,000, you don't have to risk anything to make $100,000. You have to do a lot of risking to get the million. So at a certain point it is maybe not as wise to gamble that million dollars. We're using an economic barometer, but we're not really talking about money.

I try to be as careful as I can not to expose myself needlessly, so by the time I say, "OK, let's go" with a project, that means I'm out on that high sea and there's no return. I'm going to make that other shore or I'm not going to make that other shore. It's really a risk when you're involved with your time, your work, your talent, and my God, what are those critics going to do to you? When you do creative work, there is no such thing as a sure thing, so it's all risk. That's what I'm saying: It's less wise.

At a different time in my life, I might have taken those risks despite all my doubts because I may not have had other choices. I have other choices now, so when I go with a project, I want to feel as good as I can. I want to believe in it, really believe in it. But once I believe in it, there's no question.

The more successful you are, the fewer risks you have to take: That's one of the advantages of being successful—you can minimize certain aspects of risk.

Edward McCabe, ADVERTISING EXECUTIVE

Do I not take risks because I have more to lose? No. Having more to lose makes the risk more worth taking.

Mary Boone, ART DEALER

Trusting Your Unconscious

If something seems like it's taking a form that I don't know about, I like to go with it. I guess that's something I learned in art school, the idea of trusting your unconscious.

Basically I think the gallery itself is almost like a separate entity, it has its own life that swerves and moves and undulates. I think if you say you want to go from point *A* to point *B* in a totally straight line, you would end up with as airless a result as an artist's who has a total preconception before he makes a painting. Then what's the sense of doing it? I like the sense of unexpectedness and surprise, and oftentimes I find that things become even greater than I could have imagined them. So I try to be flexible as well as having a long-range goal.

Ambitious Work

It's about investigation. I'm interested in investigation. I'm interested in learning about things. I don't want to look at something that I know about; I want to look at something I don't know about. This constant pressure to just push forward and make things greater, more ambitious in that sense—to me, that is what ambitious work is about: the quest for information.

Courage

I don't think of selecting artists as "gambling." I think of it as risk taking. I like taking risks and I like courage. If I had to say what I look for in an artist, what I look for first and foremost is courage, as exemplified by listening to yourself and discovering your own internal language. That takes a lot of intelligence, but even more courage.

I thought I had a lot to lose in the beginning and I feel I have a lot to lose now. I opened this gallery because I felt there were some artists I wanted to show who weren't being shown, a kind of vision of the world that didn't have a voice. It was important to me. I remember another dealer even saying to me, when I opened, "Boy, Mary, you're so lucky. You have nothing to lose," and I remember that statement resonating in my head and I thought, "I do have something to lose. I feel strongly about this. That means I have something to lose."

I don't think being successful makes it harder to take risks.

Milton Glaser, GRAPHIC DESIGNER

Idea and Execution

I've been teaching design for a very long time, and when you teach design, you always get to one issue that's very central, which is this form and content idea. You can always see ideas that are badly executed, where something fails because the idea was strong but the execution was weak. And you also see the opposite, where the idea is weak but the execution is strong, as when you see a dead idea or something trivial done well. In both cases, you can be impressed by either aspect. You can be impressed by the central vision and make allowances for the poor execution, or you can admire the technique of a thin idea. But the things that we truly celebrate are always those in which you cannot separate the two at all. Once you can actually separate the idea and the execution, where they're perceived as being two separate elements not harmoniously brought together, you're dealing with an incomplete work of one sort or another. In the works that impress most, those things are inseparable; you can't think of the form without the content.

It may not be as elevated as genius, but it's good to be able to reconcile those two things. Usually people tend to be stronger in one aspect than they are in the other. If you have somebody who is equally strong in both departments, you have somebody who turns out to be very effective in the world. I think I am basically able to deal with both issues. I like both.

There is something that's very life enhancing about moving things, making something, the physical act of making, where you don't know what you're doing and stumble into something. There are some things you can't think up without making.

Incidentally, that's probably one of the things that happens where you don't get the vitality of a significant work, because you do sense there is a separation between conception and making. Somebody thought of something and had it made, as opposed to having thought of something and started to make it and in the course of making it, changed it. I think the best work comes about in that latter way—when the act of doing changes the work. Work that doesn't change in the act of doing is basically a rendering and it's all finished before you start. Works that are finished before you start are not the best works.

Dr. Richard Winter, EXECUTIVE HEALTH EXAMINERS

Developing Ideas

Great ideas don't just *come* to people; you don't just sit around and say, "What's the great idea for today?" and someone says, "Well, I know what we'll do. We'll publish *The New York Times*." It just doesn't happen that way. Our *Executive Health* books were a development of a series of ideas, one leading to another, that led to the books. It's a very successful idea because the advances have been enormous, fifty thousand dollars a book.

The book thing to me was sort of a classic example of how something starts out. Today someone says, "Oh, boy, you have three books in Book-of-the-Month Club; how did you do that?" "Oh, I just sat down and created three books and Book-of-the-Month Club bought them." Baloney!

What happened actually was we raised our clinic fees. We do it every year; obviously, we have to. And the marketing people here always say that if you raise the fees you've got to give something more to the client. We needed to have something else. And if we have something else that costs a lot of money, what's the point in raising the fees? So what you really have to do is add something that's perceived as a useful addition but really costs very little.

So someone said, "I'll tell you what. We'll have a nutrition program. We'll tell the clients we're going to give them a nutrition program." Great! Go out, tell the clients. We didn't have nutrition then; nobody knew what the hell nutrition was, we figured, so we'd teach them.

So we got the fee increase, and a couple of months went by, and a couple of clients said, "Where's the nutrition program?" We couldn't really blame them for that, so I said to one of our doctors and our chief nutritionist,

"You guys better go and develop some kind of nutrition program that costs like nothing but seems to do some good." So, they develop a little manual that could be used in conjunction with the examination, ten pages of information on nutrition. It was kind of a handout to the patients, and our marketing head looked at this thing and he said, "You know, this is pretty good; I'm going to improve it." So, he rewrote it, put it in color, and rebound it. It got to be more expensive, but it was a nice product, almost like a little magazine.

What we did was, every patient that came through got one of these as part of his examination and if, for example, his cholesterol was slightly elevated, in the written report he got he was referred to page 16 of his nutrition manual, where the full description appeared. It was a nice tie-in, and the patients liked it. So I looked at this thing and I said, "I really think this could be a book; all we've got to do is fill this thing out." I asked someone in publishing to come in with us and take a look at this thing and he said, "You're absolutely right, this is great—but you know what? This can be a series, it's a library." He went over with this nutrition manual and he sold McGraw-Hill the idea for the series, and then we went out and got another writer and wrote the books, and there you are. So what I'm saying is, what started out as something to justify a fee increase ended up as an entire series of books which are found on bookshelves worldwide.

George Lang, RESTAURATEUR

Tradition vs. Innovation

Some days I feel that tradition is a kind of a conspiracy to keep anything new from happening, but sometimes I feel that without tradition, it would be like building a building without a foundation.

One of the concepts I teach in my seminars is, Try not to merchandise from weakness. What does that mean? It means that you do certain things because it's easy or you don't do certain things because it's not easy— instead of trying to find out what's the best possible.

For example, take a very prickly New York City project I'm working on with Jim Rouse, the man who started Baltimore's Harborplace and Quincy Market. In a meeting we had with city officials, everybody said, "We cannot do this because this group is not going to allow this, that group is not going to allow that," and Jim said, "Forget it, don't worry. Right now let's dream, let's think what's best, what would be best for the city of New York, for the people of New York. Don't worry right now whether it's doable or not."

Or let's say in the eighteenth century the candle manufacturers are all kinds of creative geniuses. And one of them says, "Why don't we come up with a different color candle so the housewife can buy beautiful colors?" The next one says, "Well, why don't we do it in sets, with designs?" The third one comes up with nondrip, and the fourth one comes up with something that has wonderful perfume inside. Then somebody comes and says, "Hey, is there some possibility that we just go to the wall and we push something and the light goes on?"

There is a big difference between a practical dreamer and the village idiot. You cannot allow your dream to produce diarrhea. No matter how freely you dream, there's always a little bit of control somewhere. I've gotten to the point where I think in three ways, continually, at the same time—which is not an easy thing to do—so that when I dictate, I think about: (1) what I'd love to do; (2) what probably is doable if we really push and are lucky; and (3) what the steps are. I always think in steps: What next? Who does what to whom, what's the next step. Every memo of mine, every letter, every plan that I write, every meeting: What's next? Otherwise you're just talk; you become a windbag. Most people are just organized windbags.

But what I wanted to tell you is that innovation is a very careful thing—you cannot just simply free-associate.

Edward McCabe, ADVERTISING EXECUTIVE

Before You Can Solve a Problem, You Must Invent One

I think anyone who is a bit of an overachiever—or who tries to be—always invents half the problems that they solve. I certainly do, because without it I can't get excited. So, lacking a problem, I invent one. I think that's a very common thing. Sometimes it can be destructive, of course; you have to know when it's productive and when it's destructive. It can always be beneficial if you can pull it out of the fire.

There are some people who like to keep things moving and fluid and unresolved, while I like to always push things to the wall and have everything resolved one way or another. I create confrontations where often they're unnecessary, because from these confrontations I believe progress comes. Now the danger is, if you create the confrontation and don't make it a positive thing, you're sowing the seeds of your own destruction. A lot of people who create it can't get out of it gracefully or positively and life's a constant crisis. But I believe that you have to have a succession of crises.

In our business, confrontations come with clients over advertising. They want to do this, we want to do that, and most agencies just say, "OK, let's do it the way the client wants to do it." Well, we never do that. I don't ever want to do that. Sometimes you take it right to the brink. But if your goal is to do a better job for the client and the client knows that, then that's not a problem. It becomes incumbent upon you to constantly communicate that to the client so they don't think it's just a bunch of ego: "It has to be my way or no way." They have to realize that you really are trying to do what's right for them, and then it's not a problem. It's sometimes uncomfortable, but it's not a problem.

I don't realize I'm doing it when I'm doing it, it's so gut and instinctive. I look at it in retrospect sometimes and I laugh and say, "My God, was that a dangerous thing!" I don't think these things through. I have a sense of what has to happen to make the next thing happen. I'm not always right.

I'm not sure that what I'm talking about is manipulating myself and others at all. I have a feeling that it's equally possible they're manipulating me, that they come in and say, "This is what we want to do," knowing that I'll leap over that hurdle and do something better. But they would never admit that. Maybe these are the kinds of games that people play; I don't know. I don't think about these kinds of things, I just go ahead and do it. But it's quite possible that people say, "This is how we're going to get him up for this." Ultimately it doesn't matter because what matters is what goes on the television screen, what goes in the magazine, how we all feel about it, and how successful it is.

Jerry Rubin, BUSINESS NETWORKING SALONS

Pressure May Inspire

Pressure may inspire. I know that when I'm interviewed on television, if I'm asked a friendly question by a smiling interviewer, I give a pretty bland, boring, uninteresting response. If I'm asked a challenging question by an interviewer with even a touch of hostility, I always give an inspired, brilliant response because I feel a little defensive. But this can be overdone. If a person's too hostile, then it doesn't work. Everything in moderation, with that little edge. So I do act better in confrontation than I do otherwise.

George Lang, RESTAURATEUR

Holding the Bar Higher

For a while, like somebody who receives a terrific, unexpected gift, I played with my abilities, my talents, the fact that people came to me from the most unexpected areas and levels and worlds, and I could not say no. Now, fortunately, not only have I got to the point where I've done so many things that I'm not continually frustrated anymore, but I also don't have to worry that much about next month's rent. What prompted me always to say yes was strictly the excitement of somebody holding up a bar, higher and higher, presenting more and more difficulty. Some of the bars had nails in them and some were flaming hot, and then it was an exciting thing to jump over—or make them lower it. But now I am doing less and less with more and more depth.

A very important thought should be interjected here, which is that people react differently to pressure. The second point about professional situations that have pressure is that some people create their own pressure for their own reasons. I thrive on pressure. I just absolutely fly and get on top of the world when things are getting very difficult, very complex, and other people would scream and collapse. To some degree, I suppose everybody can learn that. The brain is really nothing but another muscle, and you can train it to do almost anything, but some people have more fat and some people have less.

Very often I produce my own pressure. Whether I create it because I thrive on it, or produce it because

I'm rather casual and loose on occasion with offers to people or accepting other people's requests, I don't know. That's one of the keys to my nature.

Seeing What Others Don't

I was at the New York World's Fair, a representative of my company, from 1964–65. I lived there for a year, virtually. I'm quite a good photographer, but I did not take a single shot during the period, even though there were incredible possibilities, because there was so much of it. On the other hand, I can walk along the dullest street of the universe, there's nothing there, just bare walls with dull, uninteresting people walking by, and I have a field day.

Anybody with enough time and enough budget can create just about anything. The real talents can do it when one or the other is short.

John DePasquale, DIRECT MARKETING

Every Problem Is an Opportunity

One of the traits of being successful, as far as I'm concerned, is that one must look at every problem as an opportunity, and at every defeat as an opportunity and not as a failure. Accept it as a failure, but you must learn from it and look for the opportunity that it presents.

Milton Glaser, GRAPHIC DESIGNER

The Problem Is the Foundation for the Solution

I like that sense of facing resistance. I like it, and I hate it, but I don't move away from it. I like problems that are inherently difficult, that need to be worked around. I like the act of making the resistance a guideline for solving the issue. The nature of the problem itself—everything that is set up as a problem or a difficulty—becomes a guideline to action. Rather than think-ing of something as a wall you have to penetrate, you sort of step up over it. When you hear, "Well, you can't do this because of this, you can't do this because of that," that's great because that gives you exactly the guide you need. Very often, you just walk right through the spaces between. I love that sense. It's like if you have a sonnet form, it's easier to write than if you just write a poem, and that's true of everything I do.

Christopher Whittle, CHAIRMAN, *ESQUIRE* MAGAZINE

Upping the Ante

You always up the ante. You definitely do. And you say, "OK, fine, let's try another." *Esquire* was one of those things: "Let's go take on something that's going to be tough and hard." We did, and we're right now scratching our heads for the next one. We are interested in what the next one will be—and that doesn't mean we'll abandon the existing ones. We don't do that at all.

I'm not looking at it solely in terms of business and deals. There are different forms of upping the ante. The ante does not have to be monetary; I think the best ones aren't, meaning you can set challenges that have noth-ing to do with money. The whole *Esquire* enterprise is an example. It really was not a monetary objective. It's not the kind of magazine that makes a lot of money; we knew that all along. It is more of an editorial exercise. That doesn't mean we're totally philanthropic, but there are lots of things we could have done that would have been better financially. It represented a different form of challenge.

Another good example is what we did for the fiftieth-anniversary issue. My partner, Phillip Moffitt, was really the one who took on this challenge. What he did was put together fifty of America's best writers into one magazine issue, a significant challenge and something that had really never been done. To organize that number of noted writers into one event, from a monetary perspective, can't be profitable, but you have to look at profits in a very big sense, in its ultimate effect on the magazine. That was something he wanted to do.

I enjoy expansive moves, meaning I like to think of increasing the scale and significance. Scale is just size, increasing the reach of what you're doing. Significance is increasing the impact. It accomplishes something, whatever that might be, so I enjoy that. It motivates me. I look for those things.

George Lang, RESTAURATEUR

Managers vs. Prophets

You can divide people by many different formulas, by using different criteria. One kind useful in business are people who are very good at maintaining standards. This is no mean thing—it's a difficult, very complex thing, as in the case of a good manager, good patron, good owner. It's extremely difficult to operate one unit well. It becomes even more difficult to run more.

The creative person is in a sense a person who prophesies something. Now there are two kinds of conceptual thinkers. One is only a prophet and says, I think this is what's going to happen, even though nobody is doing it and nobody ever heard of it. The other kind, instead of taking his hat and leaving, he also says, This is how you get it done.

What makes my life exciting is that in different projects and at different levels I can dream, and then I often can be effective assisting the client to make sure that the dream will turn into a reality. Rarely is it 100 percent, but it is usually a high percentage.

John Diebold, MANAGEMENT CONSULTANT

Innovation: Looking Outside the Problem for the Solution

I don't know if one can learn to think innovatively. I suppose there are certain exercises you can go through that show you how to look outside the problem for the solution. I don't know. I think a lot of that is your innate character and your mental frame. Innovation is extremely important. The problem is, of course, creating an organization where you can have people like that but where you also have the follow-through to keep the innovation from dying. There are some people who have hundreds of good ideas and nothing ever happens with the good ideas. The problem with an organization is how to provide for the good ideas and still make sure that something happens.

It's rare to find individuals who can do both, but you've got to try to combine it. You've got to try to seed an operation with somebody like that, but have a group that can provide a sieve for the ideas and take the ones that are good and move ahead.

My strength is ideas, and new ideas, but I guess I'm very stubborn and I stay with a thing for a very long time, so that probably is some combination. I don't like to admit that an idea can't be made to work—often to a fault. But it is important to have those two; organizationally you have to do it by pairing people or by putting a person with good ideas with others who have the staying power to stay with it.

John DePasquale, DIRECT MARKETING

Changing Needs: Entrepreneurs vs. Managers

As you build and as your vision becomes more real and the physical entity begins to take shape, you have to recognize that what it takes to start something, to get it up and running, and what it takes to ensure it are different things. The biggest mistake that a lot of entrepreneurs make is that they stick with it through the maturation process and blow it because their concept is one vision and their ability is one of getting it going, and now they should turn it over to professional managers. Statistically, entrepreneurs are not professional managers. They run by the seat of the pants a lot; they go by gut. We are going through that now and I am trying to deal with that myself. I'm bringing in professional managers.

It's a very traumatic time in my life because as I look to the maturation process of our company, a number of people who have been here for years and who were important and skilled in being part of a building company have in effect reached their level of the Peter Principle. I didn't really understand what that was even when I read the book for the second time; I knew it intellectually, but you don't understand it until you see it happening in your own company. I'm having to let people go because they're not going to be able to be effective for us and for themselves as the company matures. It's better for them and better for us that they depart now before we get too far down the maturation curve. But it's really tough.

Edward McCabe, ADVERTISING EXECUTIVE

Management Is Simple Stuff

The distinction between the good manager and the entrepreneur is a fallacious one. It's always been assumed that you're good at either one or the other. It's more likely that a creative person can be a good manager than a manager can be a good creative person, because management skills are very easy to learn. It's simple stuff. You can't teach someone how to be creative in a seminar. So if I wanted to bet on who the most brilliant manager would be, I would always pick the creative people and give them management training. I wouldn't want to pick the management people and say, "OK, become a genius." I think that whole training of people who have a deep management background in a way is alien to being creative, because it's a numbers orientation. It's short-term thinking—a lot of long-term planning and short-term thinking—and it's profit motivated. You know: "The first objective of business is to stay in business." I don't believe that. I think the first objective of business is to stay in business with pride. Otherwise, I'd just as soon not be in business.

Becoming a manager became necessary for me. I suddenly realized what needed to be done and where we had to go. Creative people in the advertising business are always conflicted, saying they're doing more and more management work while they'd rather be doing more writing and they're doing less. Now that's fine, there's nothing wrong with it, and in those instances, maybe that's true, maybe they should be writing. But I'm not bothered by that. It's another challenge. Why can't I do that as well as I can write? Why isn't that rewarding?

What makes taking risks harder is that you build a company, you hire the best people you can, and you believe you're hiring in your own image—everyone does—and you find out that a lot of the people you have don't actually have the same motivation, don't have the same need to do things. This is not to put down the people that work for us. It's inevitable when you get enough people around, some will be that way. Now, how do you overcome that? That's a major challenge to a business.

We're talking about a business that started as someone's dreams—a brilliant idea in manufacturing, marketing, any area—and he went to the investors and they said it couldn't be done, and he got the financing, and then he went to someone else and they said it couldn't be manufactured, and he got it manufactured, and he surrounded himself with smart people and it became quite successful, and now there are a lot of MBA managers around with slide rules, trying to protect the empire. But the guys who made it happen aren't there anymore. That's one of the frustrations. It isn't all done through the clients' bureaucracies. It's the bureaucracy we create to match the clients' bureaucracy.

John Diebold, MANAGEMENT CONSULTANT

I always assume that once you can describe a concept, people ought to be able to understand and run with it. And they don't, of course. It takes endless time to do something, doing the obvious. That gets boring and yet it's essential, and that bothers me.

There's no question that there are certain kinds of organizations that move quite rapidly once you get across concepts, and others where it's a terrific bureaucratic process. The latter, of course, don't tend to stay around very long in today's world. But big bureaucracies are death as far as business goes.

Getting well-established institutions to change is very tough. Education is a good example. The whole field of education is one that has really used computer technology only in a peripheral way when, between TV and computers and communications and some of the other things that have been happening, you could *really* change the whole educational system monumentally, and vastly improve it and vastly increase the ability of the individual student to come out well. It's not used at all that way because of the educational bureaucracy and the difficulty of getting change through the entrenched position of the teachers. It's a tremendous bureaucratic problem. Institutions resist change.

The educational world is reactionary in terms of changes in the way you teach in a public school, for example. There's no research and development. This is true of many public services where you're delivering a very labor-intensive service. At a point in history when it's suicidal to be labor intensive, they're very labor intensive and it means the quality of the service constantly goes down, cost goes way up, and they don't take advantage of science in the delivery process. That's true of education and that's true of most government functions other than the military. It's because of the institutional characteristic.

We're a terrible bureaucracy already. It's a real problem. We do all the obvious things to fight it. The nature of what we do is the biggest precaution because we're dealing with terrific rates of change and with the cutting edge, and that in itself jars anyone here who's getting too complacent. That's important.

V. THE SUCCESS STUFF

What it means when you decide to succeed

The consensus on success is that it begins with a certain attitude toward what you do and why you're doing it. Vocation, hard work, and determination are the three factors most frequently cited as requirements for success. Vocation means you have to love what you're doing; hard work refers to the fact that success is a strenuous activity. The notion of determination is slightly more complex: It is that quality of not knowing when—or how—to give up.

VOCATION

David Brown, FILM PRODUCER

The Thing You Most Enjoy Doing

You can be born with a hundred million dollars, but unless you find something you really enjoy, money is of no consequence. I believe that you're OK if you do something you like. I've always done something I would do for nothing. I've always enjoyed what I've done.

Work Is the Central Thing

People can use their work as their hobby, their avocation, as the thing they most enjoy doing. The common strain in success is that people love what they're doing. I've seen men and women who are killing themselves and I've asked them why, and they say, Because I love it. Beverly Sills said that once when asked about it; many people have said it. I've said it.

Jeffrey Feinman, PROMOTIONAL CONSULTANT

Insanity

There's a theory called *instrumental behavior,* which says that work is what you do all day to be able to do what you really want to do at night. That's insane. If what you want to do is teach school, go ahead and teach school. It's incredible to me to spend most of your waking hours doing something you don't enjoy.

Richard Leibner, AGENT

The Most Important Thing

Eric Sevareid, a client, is someone who's taught me my whole life. Eric always says, "People complain about work. Most people are always saying, 'Where are we going on vacation? What will we do tonight?' Work's the most important thing in our lives." And it's true.

Work Keeps You Young

I started doing this at twenty-six. I'm forty-five now and I still think of myself as closer to college than to fifty, in attitude, in running around and carrying on. Walk into the office and you'll find me hanging from a coat hanger. I curse and yell and scream as a release. It's a method of keeping equilibrium. I must run five miles a day in the hallways of the office. I've been known to get up on somebody's desk in the office at one of the networks and kick the papers off. Everyone thinks I should be committed. But the days are over before they start. I argue with clients all the time: Don't just talk career to me, talk career and quality of life.

Mary Boone, ART DEALER

Workaholism

When I first started I did work long hours; I still work long hours. I'm a workaholic. It's one of my problems, actually. I love what I do; there's almost nothing I love to do more. That's a problem only because sometimes you sit and think, "I should know more about the world." I think there's a danger of being myopic when you're too focused, so in the last couple of years I've tried to expand a little.

Jeffrey Feinman, PROMOTIONAL CONSULTANT

"I'd Really Rather Be Working"

It took me a long time to get to the point where it was OK to work hard. Even the word *workaholic* is such a pejorative term. It was a great breakthrough for me to say, "I'd really rather be working than at the movies."

I still work sixteen hours a day. At the beginning you tell yourself you're working hard because you're building a business. Now I guess I'm working hard because I like it. Money has absolutely nothing to do with it. There's nothing I've ever bought that has given me any pleasure. It's just winning, proving—it's the game.

Dr. Richard Winter, EXECUTIVE HEALTH EXAMINERS

I like what I'm doing, and I love to talk business. Business takes place all day long; if I didn't have a luncheon date today I'd be out of sorts. I haven't had lunch alone in twenty years.

Otto Bettmann,   BETTMANN ARCHIVE

My avocation was always my vocation.

Jerry Rubin,   BUSINESS NETWORKING SALONS

Turn Hobbies into Business

I'm very stubborn, so I would have hung around till I succeeded, but I'm not sure I would have succeeded at anything I did. I think I chose the things I could do well. You have to connect your talents to your interests—turn your hobbies into business. Or learn to like what you can do.

This guy I knew in the sixties brought his nineteen-year-old kid to see me. I said, "What do you want to be?" He had no ambitions; I told him he ought to become an accountant. The point of that is, Change your interests to fit what counts in the world. Why lead a trivial life when you can lead an involved one?

Edward McCabe,   ADVERTISING EXECUTIVE

It Has to Be Interesting

So long as it wasn't boring, I probably would have succeeded at anything. Being a teacher would have been a problem because I didn't have the educational background. I was a high-school dropout.

This is going to sound arrogant: If I had been in any other business—and in most other businesses, making money is a much bigger motivation than it is in advertising—and if I had devoted to making money what I devoted to advertising, I'd be one of the richest men in the world today, I think. And so what? So I sometimes say, Hey, how much money do you need? What's the point? You also want to be sure it's interesting. You can't make certain things interesting. It can't be done. I don't think you can make accounting interesting. I just don't believe it. The language is numbers and numbers are a boring language—unless you're a mathematician and turned on by that. Now, being a person who isn't turned on by numbers, in any way, I would find that boring. I'm not saying they're boring, period, they're boring to me.

Mary Boone, ART DEALER

What's Natural Comes Easy

I've always found people who are well suited to their job have almost an extrasensory consciousness of every action. I think it's very much me, the job, and most of what I do I do by instinct. There's an ease about it, an intuition of what's needed.

If you're doing what you should be doing, although there's a lot of hard work, it almost comes naturally, because the desire to do well supersedes anything else. By the same token, I think you can only really excel at something you have that extra sense about.

Lois Wyse, ADVERTISING EXECUTIVE

The Right Attitude

I have a lot of enthusiasm about my work. I love the agency business. I think it's the best business in the whole world. I don't want to be in any other business, I just want to be better at this one. I'm not yet as good as I hope I'll be.

Edward McCabe, ADVERTISING EXECUTIVE

The only thing I lose sleep over is a feeling of unease that we're never as good as we should be—and that's always there. Work's not the most important thing in my life, but I don't know what is.

WORK

Lois Wyse, ADVERTISING EXECUTIVE

The Most Important Thing: Hard Work

The most important thing is to work. The most important thing is not what your title is. The most important thing is not what your salary is. The most important thing is not what you're getting from the job but what you're giving to the job. I sound very corny but that's what I really do believe. People come into jobs like prima donnas and want to know what their job satisfactions are. I just look at them.

There's not anything I won't do, and the good people here are all that way. They do what they have to do. They pitch in, they're a part of everything, just like the good members in a family. Business is the same way: You can't wait for breakfast in bed.

Just Doing What Needs to Be Done

I'll answer phones. I'll clean sinks. I'm not above anything; if it makes it all run smoother, fine. I really don't look for the glory in the job. I like to get things done. If somebody is helped by my moving in this direction instead of that direction, fine.

I don't think about failure and success; I don't sit around thinking about them. Really, the most important thing is to be willing to do anything and not be above any job. I can't think of anything else.

David Liederman, DAVID'S COOKIES

It Has to Be Work

There's a certain common sense to business. People come in here begging to open cookie stores. I'll look them in the eye and say, "Why do you want to be in the cookie business?" "Well, I have a girlfriend, a wife, a daughter, a son—they need something to do." I say, "Go away. You don't know what this is all about. You want to go into this business? This is business, like the potato business, or the steel business, or the pumping-gas business. If you want to be successful you go to work."

Everybody thinks cookies are cute. Everybody thinks you can open up a cookie store and people are going to put money in the cash register. The next thing they say is, "I've got plenty of money." Well, everybody always has plenty of money for a good idea. Money chases money. And I say, "That's not what David's Cookies is all about."

Helen Boehm, BOEHM PORCELAIN

A Four-Letter Word (Work)

Boehm porcelain is now in a hundred museums throughout the world, and hospitals, universities, the White House, Buckingham Palace. That's very important to me. It's a joy. And it's work. It's a four-letter word that does that, and I'm still working hard, and still love what I'm doing. When you work hard, things do become a reality.

When I do something, I do it with all my heart. I work hard, I play hard, I rest hard. Anyone who has an interest in life, who loves their work, does. When you're young, you can take any risk you want if you love what you're doing. How much do you need when you're young? It's so much easier when you don't have much to lose, when you don't have a wife or husband. If you don't make mistakes, you're never going to learn—you're never going to do anything.

Jerry Rubin, BUSINESS NETWORKING SALONS

All It Takes Is Work

Nothing is as important as hard work. I've worked around the clock from the sixties to the eighties. But it's not work if you make your hobby your work. I've made my hobby—meeting people, going to parties—work. In the sixties, I made my ideas my business. I was able to act on my ideas.

Hal David, SONGWRITER

The Best Way to Become Good

I like to think I'm not an envious person—or not an unduly envious person. I like to think I'm generous in wishing people well. I was a late bloomer among my peers. Some of the people I started out with wrote hits before I wrote hits. I perhaps went the furthest of all of them, but I was among the last to crack through, and it used to upset the hell out of me. I used to be ashamed that I envied them: "Why them and not me?" And I used to say to myself, "Well, maybe I don't have it," and that's a terrible feeling.

I think the fact that I was a late starter in terms of having a success among my peers made me work probably harder than any of them ever worked. I established the pattern for hard work. But you know, the best way to become good is to work at it, and I sure worked at it. Maybe if it came easier, I wouldn't have worked so hard. I think as a rule, success doesn't come overnight, and generally speaking, you're better off that way. It's better if you have that long haul—not too long—but if you have that long haul, I think you refine everything about yourself, you learn about yourself.

DETERMINATION

Jeffrey Feinman, PROMOTIONAL CONSULTANT

Willingness

The world is ready for anybody who does anything well. I think people who come to anything with the spirit of being willing to do $1.20's worth of work for $1.00 of pay will do terrifically at it.

I recently read an interview with the president of Sony, who said, "I read every American magazine and look for ideas. I'm sure there's not an American business-man who reads any Japanese magazines." The inter-viewer said, "Well, that's because they don't speak Japanese." And the president said, "Do you think it was easy for me to learn to speak English?"

I'm sure some young, hungry guy could come in and run us out of business in ninety days. All he'd have to do is give our clients a little more service, make a few more calls, be there one more late night. You have to love what you're doing, or love the money, or love the winning. People work really hard for different reasons, but there has to *be* a reason. A lot of people say, "I really want to succeed," but they're not willing to pay the price.

There Are No Bargains at the Success Counter

The best advice I ever got was when I first started this business and I was flying to Chicago and got bumped from coach to first class. I sat next to the chairman of the board of a steel company, and he said to me, "Young man, there are no bargains at the success counter." It's true. If you're willing to pay the price, it's out there; if you're not, that's OK, too.

You're Responsible

What I'm preaching is, Figure out what you want to do and then go do it. If what you want to do is watch *I Love Lucy* reruns and eat bonbons, then do that. I haven't met anyone who's "made it" working ten to four. They may be out there, but I sure haven't met them.

I don't preach that that is what everyone should do. People should do what feels good. But you shouldn't bullshit anyone that you really want to be great at business but that people are taking advantage of you. You're responsible.

It's Practice, Not Genius

I've always had this theory that there's nothing very hard about business. It's not like medicine or law—it's really a matter of being willing to put in a lot of hours. I have that theory about most things, that it's really more practice than genius.

George Lang, RESTAURATEUR

Always Do a Little More

The ones who succeed are the ones who always do a little more and a little better than is required. The first kitchen I worked in, I stayed after a backbreaking nine or ten hours—two hours free between lunch and dinner—I stayed sometimes four or six hours after that to see how other people were doing things. I used to come in early to see how the soup man operated. I used to bug the hell out of the chef's secretary to let me look at the book of different recipes. I used it like a college, a place to study.

Lois Wyse, ADVERTISING EXECUTIVE

Always Say Yes

I have always said to my daughter, "Always say yes, because nothing ever happens to girls who say no." It's true in business and it's true in life. "Will you stay late and work?" If you say no, nothing good is going to happen to you. "Can you take this extra assignment?" If you say no, *nothing* is going to happen to you. The only way anything happens is when you say yes. You have to learn to say "Yes."

David Brown, FILM PRODUCER

Always Say Yes . . . and Mean It

One dictum about success that worked for me, being a Depression child, was that I was always willing to take on more than one job. Therefore, when magazine staffs were being cut back and when organizations were being decimated by the Depression, I would do everything: I'd be on the switchboard, I'd do everything.

I always worked at being scared; I'm still scared. I worked at doing more, and therefore in my middle twenties I became editor-in-chief of the third largest magazine in the country, *Liberty Magazine.*

When I came back from the army I was entitled to have my old job at *Liberty* back under the GI Bill of Rights. But they didn't have my old job, which was articles editor. The editor then said, "David, we don't have your old job. But we do have the fiction job open." I said, "I don't know anything about fiction, but I'll take it." And he said, "One more thing. We don't have an office; you'll have to work in the reception area." I said, "That's OK." So I learned about fiction. I started reading short stories and novels. I was reading manuscripts in the reception room.

This is the point about success: When the big contraction came, I was the only man or woman on the staff who had done both articles and fiction and therefore I was qualified to be editor-in-chief. I knew about fiction; that's what got me my job with Darryl F. Zanuck, because I was buying the stories that movies were made from.

Upon arriving in Hollywood, I found depression. It was like being back at *Liberty Magazine.* There was a period of enormous contraction. This was late 1951. Television was coming. The movie industry was as paralyzed by it as it had been by the advent of talking pictures. I was brought out as managing editor of the story department by Darryl Zanuck. Within weeks, I was in charge of hiring producers, writers, dialogue coaches. I made all the deals. Yes, I was scared, but no more scared than when the publisher of *Liberty Magazine* said to me, when I was in my twenties, "Can you edit this magazine? You're such a baby; do you really think you can edit this?" I said, "Yeah, I can edit this magazine." I didn't know.

At the studio they fired everybody and I was willing to do all the work. I don't know if they ever asked me— I just did it. And so I got to do just about everything at Twentieth Century-Fox, eventually winding up as executive vice-president and a member of the board of directors.

Jeffrey Feinman, PROMOTIONAL CONSULTANT

You Are or You Aren't

Even though we're in the incentive business, I really don't believe in incentives. By that I mean you can't dock the switchboard operator for coming in late or reward her extra money for coming in early. She's either the kind of person who comes on time or she's not.

We've had switchboard operators who floated in at 9:30 A.M. We don't get mad, we don't get crazy. What we say is, "*We* start at nine o'clock," and she'll say, "Oh, the train, my brother, the this, the that." What we say is, "Look, we appreciate all that. What you ought to do is go someplace where they start at ten o'clock. We'll help you find that job."

We tend to find people who are as crazy as we are and who are into the whole game. The people who are key players here are all like that. You can come in here on a Saturday or Sunday and not necessarily find me, but find other people. You'll always find someone here at 7:00 in the morning. You go to the American Express building at one minute after 5:00 P.M. and you can get killed because of the people pouring out.

The Extra Mile

I just had an incident with a salesman who had a problem with one of his accounts. I asked him to return from Key West, where he was vacationing, and see the client to put the client's mind at ease. He said, "Oh, there's only one flight a day," etcetera. I said, "Look, just so we're clear and don't bullshit each other, there are connecting flights and ways to do it. If I said, 'If you're there at noon tomorrow, I'll give you one hundred thousand dollars,' would you be there?" He said, "Yes." So I said, "What you want to tell me is it's not important enough to you to see the client, which I can accept, but let's not con me or con yourself that you can't make flight arrangements." It's being willing to go the extra mile, and most people are not. Doing everything you're told to do is just not enough.

Nolan Bushnell, ATARI

It Will Happen

It's being unwilling to embrace the concept of failure, and saying "I don't know how much is enough. If I give it all I've got, then that's got to be enough. This *will* happen. I will force this to happen. It will happen."

It's the difference between being a passenger and being the pilot. I'm willing to say that if there's a random pilot, I will take random odds that I'm going to have the same statistics as everyone else. If I'm the pilot, based on my own self-confidence and my knowledge of the risks I'm willing to take and the way I'm looking at it, my piloting is going to change the odds. There are an awful lot of businesses that have failed because of people not doing it right. I may not start out right, but I'm going to learn fast enough that I'm going to be able to do it right, and therefore change the odds overwhelmingly in my favor.

I've been discouraged, yes. Hopeless, no. Exhausted, yes. You keep going by saying there's always a solution to any problem: Let's find it.

Helen Boehm, BOEHM PORCELAIN

Scarlett O'Hara

I've built a little monster—a nice monster, but a demanding one. You have to have the desire. If you don't have the dream and the desire, it's never going to happen. And you can't just wish it'll fall into your hands. You can't spend your time envying or thinking about twenty years from now; just do your best today and tomorrow will come. But don't delay anything that you can do today. You've got to clear the slate today because tomorrow's going to be a busy day, a happy day.

I'm not like Scarlett O'Hara: "I'll worry about it tomorrow." I get through it today. Tomorrow I might be needed at the White House, or have to fly to Saudi Arabia, or my polo team might need me in England.

George Lang, RESTAURATEUR

Don't Look Up

Sir Henry Morton Stanley had a bit I always remember. In one of his books or perhaps in an interview, he was asked wasn't he frightened of this incredible, horrifying jungle that no one had ever gone through? He said, "I didn't think about it that way; I did not raise my head to see the whole. I only saw this rock ahead of me; I only saw this poisonous snake in front of me, which I had to kill to take the next step. I only saw the problem directly in front of me. Only after I had gotten through the whole thing did I look back and see the whole of what

I had been through. If I had taken a look at the whole thing I would have been so scared that I would never have attempted this."

Lois Wyse, ADVERTISING EXECUTIVE

You can do anything you want to do; the time is there. I don't believe *I* can do anything, but I think I can try anything. No, I don't think I'm going to be successful at everything I do, but I want to try it. I want to give it my best shot. Every experience makes me grow; I learn something out of every experience. I'm really not afraid of anything. I'm not at all afraid of failing.

Wally "Famous" Amos

Following Through on Ideas

One day the thought occurred to me that everything starts with a thought. There's nothing that you can touch, see, feel, that did not start with a thought that somebody had. So, hell, why not have some good thoughts, why not follow through on those thoughts? But people can the thought and say, "Well, I'll never be able to do that." How do you know? You haven't even tried. You *can* do it. Believe that you can do it. It's so important to believe in yourself. Believe that you can do it, under any circumstances. Because if you believe you can, then you really will. That belief just keeps you searching for the answers, and then pretty soon you get it.

Jeffrey Feinman, PROMOTIONAL CONSULTANT

How Will You Know if You Don't Try?

It crossed my mind every day to give up, especially since at that time I had other options. But I guess the other side of it was that those options would always be there, in six months or a few years. I could always go out and get "a job." The saddest thing to me are the would-have-could-have-should-have people who are fifty-three years old and say, "Boy, I should have done that." And I said, "If I don't make it"—and that was a possibility, although I never really admitted it out loud—"at least I could say I gave it my best shot."

Wally "Famous" Amos

Success Is a Journey

I read a great saying once: "Success is a journey, not a destination." You can't say, "One day I will be—." You don't know what you're going to be, you don't know where you're going to go. Life has so many detours. Be prepared to go with each and make it good. Make it something that will really benefit you.

A year from now I could be doing anything. I don't have any preconceived ideas about what I'm going to be doing; I don't know what God has planned for me, but whatever it is, it's going to be great, and I'm going to give it the best shot I've got.

Life is self-generating, and we each have the potential, we each have the creativity to do whatever we want to do. And we also have a lot of choices. We have free will. No one *makes* you do anything. I really believe that you can choose whatever life you want. It's up to each individual. You can't blame anybody but yourself. You can't blame Reaganomics, none of that stuff. Nobody.

Jeffrey Feinman, PROMOTIONAL CONSULTANT

There Are Two Kinds of People in the World . . .

My experience has generally been that there are two kinds of people in the world: There are people who get

things done and there are people busy attempting ↳
things done. If you think about the book business
whole idea that it takes five weeks to typeset a boo ⌐ ↳
insane; the idea that it takes a year to publish a book
when *The New York Times* can publish overnight is proof
of the mind-set people have wired up that this is how
long a thing takes to do, and so they make it take
that long.

Christopher Whittle, CHAIRMAN, *ESQUIRE* MAGAZINE

Just Get Out There and Do It

Successful people get legal approval later. I so take
decisiveness for granted that I don't even know I have
it. When I was twenty-two, an older guy said to me, "Just
get out there and do whatever it is. You have to push
on, and you have to recognize that it's not going to be
perfect, as much as you'd like it to be, but that it is going
to *be*." We just put into effect a whole new reward system in our company, and it's the kind of thing accountants and lawyers could spend years dabbling with the
details, and I just went, "Enough. We're going to do
this," and we did it. And they'll pick up the pieces later.

Nolan Bushnell, ATARI

Quit Reading Books

Just do it. Quit reading books. Get out and do it tomorrow. Identify first steps, and execute. Execute today. Execute them within the next hour, and don't worry
so much whether they're the right steps. The fear of
taking the wrong first step can paralyze you. So just start
taking steps, and pretty soon you'll zero in on it. But if
you spend four months trying to decide what the first step
is, you've missed it. Start stepping.

Edward McCabe, ADVERTISING EXECUTIVE

People who don't do anything are totally aware of everything they do, and people who do things aren't aware of it at all until afterward and they look back and realize what they've accomplished. People say, "Well, this is our strategy and we're going to do this, then we're going to do this," and it's all very careful. They never do anything.

Richard LaMotta, CHIPWICH

There Is Always a Way

People said to me, Was there only one low point? I said, What? *One?* There were like 450 low points, where you sort of have to put your boots back on and say, Man, I got to go out there again and take that first step, and I force myself to go back out there.

That's where the creativity comes. You've constantly gotta think.

People used to come in to me with problems, and I'd tell them, don't come to me with problems—come to me with solutions. There's a solution to every problem. Don't come in to me and say, Well, we can't do this. OK, fine. How do you get around that? How do you work it out? What can you do instead? Don't just sit there and say, Woe is me, we can't do it. I don't want to hear that. *Be creative.* Find another way, because there is always a way. God bless America for that. This is the magnificence of this country. *There's always a way if you're willing to work hard enough and stay with it,* and don't wallow in the mire and all of the muck, which is so easy to do.

We all sit back and say, Oh, I wrote my first play and they didn't like it. So what? Get out and write another one, and go to ten people, and if ten people don't like it, go to twenty, then get to fifty. Until you're totally exhausted with it, and then write a new book. Because it was obviously not the right one or the right time. But there's no such thing as luck. It's always, "Oh, you gotta be lucky." That's nonsense. You make your own luck. I do not believe in luck. There was no luck involved in Chipwich. I made everything happen. You *be* at the right place at the right time. OK? It's not a matter of timing. The timing is: You be there. Keep intersecting that line. Keep knocking your head against the wall.

Jeffrey Feinman, PROMOTIONAL CONSULTANT

You're Responsible

Years ago I used to go out with a girl who was an Olympic ice skater and what drove her crazy was when people said, "I wish I could skate like that!" She used to skate sixteen to eighteen hours a day! Luck unquestionably plays a part—and if luck turned against me, I know that as quickly as I made this money, I could lose it—but people really spend a lot of time conning themselves because they want to set up this belief system that somebody else is doing it to them—their mother, their boss. I always knew that I was doing it to myself, and frequently I *did* do it to myself, but I knew that I was responsible.

Hal David, SONGWRITER

Going the Distance

You've got to have a sense of honesty about yourself. The hardest thing, and perhaps it's the most important thing, is being honest with yourself, and that's not as easy as it sounds. To know deep down what we all know. We know when we're faking and we know when we're doing it. We may cover ourselves and we may kid ourselves, but there's something back here, I think with every one of us, and we know there's something a little better we can do. When something tells you that you have a little more, something better, just listen to that voice. I don't always do it. I probably lie to myself, too, but I try not to.

Edward McCabe, ADVERTISING EXECUTIVE

Priorities

You just keep your mind on what you're doing, on what matters.

People everywhere are always complaining about the size of their office compared to someone else's. The way I look at offices is, the biggest offices are the ones the best work comes out of. I don't notice the measurements—you have either a big office or a small office, based on what you do. A lot of people don't see things that way.

VI. EVIDENCE TO THE CONTRARY

Examples of how the right attitude can accomplish the impossible; a lot of determination goes a long way

BREAKTHROUGHS

Nolan Bushnell, ATARI

Out of Desperation Came Video Games

There was a point when I had decided that the economics of video games was not right, because I was going to use a large fixed computer with several terminals around it, and my idea then was to go strictly to the amusement-park industry. The economics of the thing worked very well at six terminals and was getting marginal at four. It started looking like I was running out of computer time at four, so I was going to have to reduce it to three, and three did not make economic sense; you couldn't get a big enough payback. So in order to keep it at four, I had to make the terminals smart enough. Then all of a sudden I said, "Hey, I don't need that big computer. I'm just going to make a very, very special smart terminal." Now I had one machine that would stand all by itself. That was the real breakthrough. Then the economics swung so heavily back that instead of being slightly more expensive than any other game in the amusement park—but giving better value, more intense graphics—it was giving those intense graphics *more cheaply* than a typical mechanical game. So that sort of despair and difficulty forced me into the right solution, which sounds now like a simple solution.

There always is a way.

Jeffrey Feinman, PROMOTIONAL CONSULTANT

It's No Big Deal

A client came to us and wanted to do a decorating book as a promotion that they would give away free with a purchase. They wanted a price at twenty thousand copies, so we called the publishers and they said, "That's forty-three percent off." I said, "Wait a minute, if I wanted to buy *six* copies it'd be forty-three percent off. This is America: The more you buy the more the price is supposed to go down." They said, "Well, we're not really set up for it. We'd have to buy trees and convert them to paper," and they made it into a whole big deal. So I thought, "Why don't we go into the book business?" Because there's nothing to the book business, it's type and writing and whatever. So we started to do books.

The first year we were in the book business we did something like eight million paperback books, more than any publisher. At a cocktail party one night, somebody said to me, "Why don't you do trade books?" I said, "What's a trade book?" I'd been in the book business about three years at that point. Then I found that editors buy ideas the same way promotion people buy ideas. In many cases, we ended up taking the clients' promotion ideas and we would hold back the trade rights, so we would do the premium book for McDonald's and the trade book for Doubleday. The clients were looking for something they could buy for a quarter that looked like two and a half dollars. Clearly the way to do that was to manufacture something out of paper, as in printing a book, because it had a ten-time markup.

We do everything. We buy the paper, hire the writer, do the research, come up with the idea, do the art, print it, ship it. We've done that for publishers as well, where they needed a book in a week and they're used to doing a book in a year. When *est* got hot, they wanted somebody to go through the training, write a book, edit it, and have finished books out in ten days. We did it.

David Liederman, DAVID'S COOKIES

Staring at the Wall

When I started buying Lindt chocolate, I bought it like everybody else. I bought it in cases, but it was wrapped up in wrappers. I personally spent hours every day unwrapping Lindt chocolate bars till I was getting dizzy in the face. So I called up the guy who was in charge of production at the plant in Zurich. And I said, The chocolate's wonderful but send me the chocolate unwrapped. He couldn't do that. I asked him why he couldn't do this: because this is the way he'd always done it, so how was he supposed to do it any other way? So I was faced with the possibility of having to stop using Lindt. So I went home one night, I stared at the wall. I was thinking about how we could solve this problem, given the intransigence of the Swiss.

Then it occurred to me. I called him up the next day, and I said, "What kind of machine do you make the chocolate bars in?" And he said, "It's a very complicated machine. The stuff is molded, it goes through a place, and it goes through another place, and it's wrapped in the tinfoil and it goes through another place and it's wrapped with the other wrapper." I said, "I have an idea. Don't load the machine with the paper." So he said, "Let me try it." So it was the same process, but the chocolate bars came out unwrapped.

It saved my sanity, probably.

I find that if I can't find a piece of equipment that works

for me, I'll invent it, or else I'll try to invent it. I'm not always successful.

You can't believe you can't; you have to try. I'm serious about that. You have to try. You just go out and keep trying. There's always a way to do something.

Edward McCabe, ADVERTISING EXECUTIVE

The biggest quality in successful people I think is an impatience with negative thinking. They just don't want to know. People look at you like you're crazy; they don't understand that.

I Did What I Had to Do

I had never thought about working for myself. I had never thought about being in the advertising business. I've never thought about anything I ever did. It's worked out fine because I felt I had to make it work. I was in a position where I couldn't choose. I was a high-school dropout. I started in a factory. I hated the heat and the dirt and the filth, so I decided I needed another job. The employment agent said, "We can't give you a job, you don't even have a high-school diploma." I thought, "Well, I'll lie about it," so I went to another employment agency and said, "I have a high-school diploma." They sent me to the mailroom in an advertising agency. They said, "You'll never get anywhere in advertising without a college degree." I said, "Well, OK, I'll go to college nights." Now, I couldn't go to college nights because I didn't have a high-school diploma. So what I did was, I started doing my homework on the thing I was involved in and making the most of that until I one day went up to the guy and said, "Look, I've written all these ads in the last year." He said, "You can't write ads; you don't have a college degree." So I went to another company, where they didn't know that, and I said, "I've written all these ads," and they assumed if I'd written ads I had a college degree. They didn't bother to ask. I learned some more, and so it went.

You know what it is? I did what I had to do. Every time. I never really thought about it.

I had no right to be in the advertising business. I had no right to be a writer. It was all wrong, it was all accidental, and I made the most of the situation as it came.

Refusing to Admit the Impossible

Many people in the beginning, even among my own associates, didn't believe that Frank Perdue could be spokesman for his own advertising and neither did Frank Perdue, because he had no experience at it and he wasn't convinced he'd be good at it. I was totally convinced. I never had any doubts, because my attitude was, "If he can't do it, I'll *make* him do it." And he did it. I mean, there are impossible things. I wish I could find one, then I might give up.

What Have You Got to Lose?

I didn't want to have my own agency. In the beginning I said, "This is the least likely partnership that anyone could imagine." I could think of eighty reasons why it wouldn't work. On the other hand, I'm sure that most of the people who don't do anything with their lives can find eighty reasons why it wouldn't work. So my feeling was, Even if it's as bad as I think it is, we'll make it work. I said, "How many opportunities come along? If you wait for the right one, that's wrong, because it may never be right, and what have you got to lose? Even if it's a disaster, you've tried, you've learned something, you've had an adventure. And that doesn't mean you can't do it again."

George Lang, RESTAURATEUR

On Innovation

We were opening Café des Artistes in 1975, and I had everything except the dessert. I could not come up with a concept and I said, "My God, everybody is expecting miracles from me. I have to have at least two or three pastry chefs and I have no space, either, it's a little, tiny, miserable basement kitchen. What am I going to do? I cannot put this on the payroll; a decent pastry chef gets forty thousand dollars. And you have to have a helper for him, and the space. There was no way on God's earth this place could afford it."

One morning I got up, and of course I was thinking about the merchandising of the place, and even though I knew that I would have people from the East Side and Beverly Hills and London, I still kept saying—for a very shrewd, I hope, merchandising reason—that this is a very simple place, just a neighborhood restaurant, because if I were to say it's a real elegant place, then it's a different kind of approach when people come. So I say, No, it's just a neighborhood kind of place, and they come and they find something which is charming. It's a wonderful reaction.

And suddenly I said, "Hey, the word *neighborhood*!" Neighborhood, neighborhood. I called in everybody. I said, "OK, guys, let's figure out how we get in touch with everybody who knows how to bake within a fifteen-block area"—which is a lot of people. Housewives, students, anybody. We started organizing so that people could bring in samples. Some days we have twenty-five cakes and tortes here, for weeks and weeks. What I'm saying is, the solution would have been to have a simple pastry shop, to have a complicated pastry shop, or to buy the stuff somewhere. Everybody's been doing that since time began. I came up with a fourth solution—that the neighbors bake it for me in their own kitchens. I don't have to worry about the space, and it's really home-baked.

John Diebold, MANAGEMENT CONSULTANT

Of Course You Can

In the very beginning, people said you couldn't work for companies that built computers or automation and their customers as well, and I felt from the beginning that one should work for both. We got our first assignment for a company building equipment. They said, Well, of course you're like an ad agency, you can't work for a competitor, and I thought that was a lot of nonsense. Now we work for essentially all the major computer and telecommunications companies in this country and Europe, and several in Japan, as well as heavily for their customers. It's an example of the point where people say, "Explain logically why you can't do both," and then why you can't do the three things, why you can't work for a competitor.

I've felt—and history proves this—the advice we've given to a variety of competitors has always been unique advice to that individual firm, and there's not been a conflict.

Richard LaMotta, CHIPWICH

There's Always a Way

I got a little marketing and advertising company and I told them what I was going to do with Chipwich, and they told me that it takes anywhere from $15 million to $25 million to do a successful introduction of a product at the retail level in the United States. And I said, $25 million! Huh, $24.5 million shy.

Then what did I do? I was walking around Manhattan

one day. They had all these street vendors, and I said, Wow, kind of a sleazy industry. Gotten a lot of bad write-ups. Not healthy—ants and roaches and the guys are filthy and their carts are bent-up and dirty. Just not very appetizing—unless you're going to have a frank that's been boiled to death.

I looked around and I said, That's it, there's my hook. I've got my marketing niche. I'll start a renaissance in street-cart vending as a new marketing technique. Not only will it be my marketing technique, but it's a great place to do test sampling. A great billboard industry. It's a great sales technique, if I handle it right.

I remembered back to my days in Coney Island when I was a hawker, when I was working my way through school. I learned how to pitch the people. I let them have a little bit of fun, a smile, and bring a little humanity to the game. That's really what it was. It's, Hi, how ya doin' today? Wanna play the game? Come on in, let me show you how much fun this is to lose two dollars to me. And make people laugh.

I said, Wow, I could bring that to the street, because these guys are standing out there like they're stiffs. There's nobody that's ever put a new face on street-cart vending. I'm going to be the one. I'm going to introduce my product that way.

There's my idea. Dress it up. Make it appealing. I'm going to make it look as good as the product. I have a premium product. I am going to try to turn an industry that's not known for selling premium products into a premium-product seller.

How do you do it? The umbrella. The graphics. The uniform. Clean, bright, smiling. The safari hat. The orange bow tie. Teach them those little entrepreneur secrets that I learned. Make that their business. Get them out there to say hello to people, whether they buy or not. Hello, how are you today? Let me show you my little magic trick, let me juggle, let me entertain you. And that's the way we're going to introduce it, because it's the only thing I can do.

And I said, Well, then I'll do it with a big bang. Boom! Sixty carts, all of a sudden, May 1, on the streets. I spent a year getting this whole act together.

John DePasquale, DIRECT MARKETING

Problems Are Really Opportunities

We had a major conflict of interest. My biggest account was American Express, had been for seven years. They came to me and said, "You folks are going to have to give up one of your accounts, Citibank." At Citibank we just had one or two small projects; American Express was, at that time, probably 75 percent of our profits. It had bothered me very much that so much of our profit came from one source. I tried everything I could to reduce the percentage of our profits that that particular account was. We were doing a pretty good job of eroding their power, but it was hard because we had that business locked in, it was efficient. Even though we had a lot of other clients, we were learning those businesses as we were going along, so even if they were bigger jobs they were not as profitable because the American Express stuff was automatic. Understand, it was simply dictum by American Express top management that anybody working for Citibank could not work for American Express.

I said to myself, I've gone this far to build my own independent company so that I can call my own shots. If I say yes to this I might as well ask American Express to buy the company because in effect they're running it and not owning it. But on the other hand, what am I going to do? I've got all this overhead and everything else and these guys are 75 percent of my profits. I said, Well, I've got to decide whether I'm in this for the long haul or not. I said, I like the business. I cannot give up having the decision-making power of how my company's going to go. So I went back and I said, "No, I will not give up Citibank business."

I sat back and I said, How do you make this very major problem into an opportunity? Survival was at stake. So I said, you've got to look for something different, you've got to look for something new. I said, Let's look at the industry that our clients are in: banking.

BankAmericard had changed its name to VISA. Wow, what an opportunity. You want to get into the BankAmericard business but you're dancing around because you hate to have your biggest competitor, Bank of America, have their name on your plastic. I said, That would bother me, too. But now you've got an opportunity: Use it.

Then it hit me. Duality. This was the first time that banks had the opportunity to offer both cards. No one had any experience in this, no one really knew. So, with a certain amount of guts, and a certain amount of gamble on our part and a certain amount of gamble on Citibank's part, we did the first program ever in the United States offering in one mailing both VISA and Master Charge, a very successful program. We rolled that out almost like a syndicated package to around ten or twelve different banks.

We did what amounted to forty million pieces, the largest mailing in the history of banking. The response was outrageous. In the course of about eighteen months they went from zero to the second largest Visa card-holding bank in the United States. With those programs we replaced whatever we lost from American Express and then some. Today we have the largest direct-response market of banks in the country. We've kept that focus all along.

Saying no to American Express was probably among the best decisions I've ever made, although at the time I didn't know that. So now I had something else to watch in this sort of input-output chart you have to guide your business by, and that is, the business of your client. Not just the economics, but details; details are what make the world go round.

Now we had the same problem we had before, but it's called Citibank instead of American Express. Citibank was so big, that they were beginning to be a dangerous percentage of our business. So we said, The only way out of this is to get into other things. So I dedicatedly went out on a limb to hire a few other people who were nonbankers, non–bank marketers, and we set about branching out in other businesses. We wanted to just sidestep from banking into other financial services, brokerage, insurance. We were methodical: Take what you know and just move a little bit to the side; don't get too far away. If you get good at that, then move a little more.

VII. OTHER BASIC REQUIREMENTS

A wide-ranging list of what it takes to succeed

John DePasquale, DIRECT MARKETING

A Host of Qualities for Success

In order to succeed, you must be driven, you must have a mission. You may not even know what that mission is, but you've got to be driven toward the goal. Your willingness to work hard has almost got to be insatiable. When I say work hard, that is not a workaholic. There are people who work ten hours a day and they're workaholics. There are people who work fifteen hours a day and they aren't workaholics. I work fifteen, sixteen hours a day now; I used to work eighteen to twenty hours a day. Now I work five, six days a week; I used to work seven days a week. But to me, work isn't work.

Optimism

The motivation, the mission, the drive—you can't teach those things. You either have them or you don't. I don't know if you're born with it, but the basic success orientation is part of an individual. Really, it's having an optimistic attitude. I don't think you can be successful if you're not basically optimistic. You can't be pessimistic, because there are so many things that go wrong every day that if you were to be negative or pessimistic, you'd go out of business. So you have to be basically an optimistic personality.

Liking Yourself

To some extent, you have to be your own best friend because nobody else is. You have a lot of friends when you're successful, but you'd be surprised where your friends go. You spend more time with yourself than anybody else in the world, so you better like yourself.

I Think I Can

You've basically got to have the intestinal fortitude of self-confidence even under conditions of strain and pressure. A lot of people under strain and pressure lose their confidence. You've got to have that get-up-and-go. It's like the little engine that could: "I think I can, I think I can," and you eventually do. You can't be shut off at the first negative.

Wally "Famous" Amos

Being Receptive to Ideas

It was not a calculated plan to go into the cookie business. For years I made chocolate-chip cookies just as a hobby. People had always suggested to me that I go in business, that I open my own store. "You ought to sell this cookie." "I know, I know." How do you go about selling chocolate-chip cookies?

But then I was receptive. You have to be ready to accept something. There are many things that are just glaring at you for years and you're not in the right frame of mind to do them, and then all of a sudden, one day, someone comes along and says, "Hey, do this." "Oh, yeah. Why didn't I think of that before? Why didn't I do that before?" Because it wasn't right before, and it was right when it was right.

You've always got to be doing things. You've got to be open, you've got to be receptive. You can't just sit down and wait for something to come to you; you have to be exploring, you have to be always in action, in the mainstream of life. People are reclusive, or they want somebody to give them something. You've got to be giving yourself, because the ideas are there. I think that the whole concept of ideas is like tuning into a radio station. Like WOR. It's there, on the band, on the frequency, but you got to tune into it. But when you go away it's still there.

Presto, I'm Successful

People got to have confidence in themselves. A lot of people don't think they can do anything. They see people who have achieved some level of success, and they say, "Oh, he was lucky, he was this, he was that." That's jive. We all start out the same as babies. We all have our evolution and our growth, but it's not just "Presto, I'm successful." It's a lot of hard work. The successful people have paid their dues, they've put in a lot of time, and been very responsible, very concerned about making things happen. I think that people have to know that they, too, can do it.

The one thing my success says more than anything is that if I can do it, anybody can do it. I was born in Tallahassee, Florida, moved to New York at twelve, high-school dropout—nobody taught me how to promote. One thing just kind of led to another. I had no special privileges. It never occurred to me that I would one day work for myself; I never thought about it. You don't know where you're going, you don't know what the destination is.

George Lang, RESTAURATEUR

Serious People

Successful people are terribly, terribly serious about what they are doing. Which means that they learn everything about their craft they can, they keep up with the learning, and they read and learn and listen continually. They keep trying to improve themselves. They realize that unless they do something different they get into a rut.

They all realize that relating to people and dealing with people is probably the most important part of the whole thing, because no matter how brilliant you are or how many terrific ideas you have, unless you can sell yourself, they won't listen to it and they won't take it.

They realize that the only deal that is good is a deal that is good for every member of the deal, everybody. So if the deal is too good, I don't think either of them would like it very much, because they know that somewhere along the line it's not going to work.

Without question, with anybody I've dealt with who's succeeded, I could say that their word is as good as their handshake; and their word and handshake were as good as a written contract.

You know what the real key is? I think that probably most everybody I've dealt with and whom I admire was able to come up with a simple, basic common-sense truth that others did not, and they were able to recognize it and apply it.

Helen Boehm, BOEHM PORCELAIN

ABC's

I guess it was the "ABC's"; my husband, Ed Boehm's ability, the breaks that came our way, and courage to enter and stay in a field, porcelain, that had always been monopolized by European and Asian companies. I had all of Europe and Asia to compete with.

Jerry Rubin, BUSINESS NETWORKING SALONS

You've Always Got to Be Able to Change

People who are stuck in one mode of how they do things might not be successful because only reality is reality; what goes on in your head has nothing to do with reality. And reality is the truth, so you better always be ready to adapt to reality.

Everything has a positive side—*you always have to look for the positive thing in everything.* That's another thing about success. I think I realized early that whenever anything happens to you, there's always something positive happening at the same time and you have to put your attention on that, and forget the negative. Just blot it out. 'Cause there's a positive thing, no matter what it is.

David Brown, FILM PRODUCER

Ambition and Power

You have to be ambitious, even though you might not get what you want. Ambition is looking for the next job, the next rung on the ladder, getting more—I hate the word *power,* but I guess it is a good word if you're saying power to legislate your own life. I've never felt settled where I was, to this very day. Never. Never have I felt that that was it. I have never felt I had a sinecure.

Richard LaMotta, CHIPWICH

If you don't have the obsession, you aren't going to make it.

Nolan Bushnell, ATARI

Damn the Torpedoes

I just saw that there was a games business out there and I wanted to address it. It was a scary plunge, but I figured I was young and resilient and I had an engineering degree. Damn the torpedoes. I had the benefit of an easy interim step. I was able to market the concept and they hired me to put it into place. The company I'd done that with was relatively poorly managed. It gave me the confidence to say, "These guys are real turkeys. I can't screw it up any more than they are, and they're doing OK." Working for incompetents is a major motivator for an entrepreneur, because the entrepreneur can say, "If this company can be successful based on these turkeys, anything's possible."

I think one of the things that has made Silicon Valley successful is that there are an awful lot of people who know two or three or four multimillionaires, and they're able to measure their own capabilities against this millionaire and say, "If he can do it, so can I."

John Diebold, MANAGEMENT CONSULTANT

Strength in Your Convictions

I never had any question whatever about the idea of automation. My judgment has always been excellent and the only times I've made mistakes have been when people argued me out of something, when very much brighter people argued me out of a position I believed to be correct.

Having strength in your convictions is very important, I think, particularly in early days in a field that's only beginning, because otherwise, the conventional wisdom drives you out of it for all sorts of reasons.

For a long time, one of the errors I regularly made was letting people argue me out of something. I'm not logical. It took me a long time to learn that my judgment was extremely good, and that all the real errors have always been when I followed someone's logical argument rather than my own judgment, which would be arrived at in part intuitively, in part by some external experience, in part by some logical thinking. If it comes down to the wire, there's no question that if I feel strongly something is right, it's what I do.

Hal David, SONGWRITER

Cultivating Talent

I think with great songwriters, with "great" anything, there's a certain gift involved, but I think you must cultivate that talent. I don't think Irving Berlin or Richard Rodgers just simply stayed with this gift they were given. They cultivated it in one way or another, they refined the sense of craftsmanship that goes with the gift. Perhaps some people who never achieve what they could achieve have that raw, wonderful gift, but don't have whatever else it takes to refine talent.

Refining Talent

I think, first, there's that great sense of determination you must have. The determination to finish today's work today; years from now you will be what you've accumulated over these twenty years.

Determination is important because it's just got to get written. It can't be put off. It won't do it by itself. There are people out there—whatever it is, whether it's for a film or a play or a pop song—that you've got to submit that work to, especially if you're climbing up the ladder, so you can get out and do the next thing. So it's got to get done.

Discipline

Discipline is very important in everything you do in your life. I always had discipline because I had to have it: Now I've been disciplined for so many years it's just second nature. To be *undisciplined* is difficult for me. I had to earn a living. There was just no way out of it.

David Brown, FILM PRODUCER

Drive. It's always drive . . . plus talent.

Nolan Bushnell, ATARI

I think the "entrepreneurial personality"—wanting to make it on his own, to make his own mistakes—is largely a myth. I think that there are as many different kinds of entrepreneurs as there are entrepreneurs, and that an awful lot of them really are so success-driven that they're willing to do whatever's necessary to make it a success.

David Liederman, DAVID'S COOKIES

People make their own luck. I don't believe in luck.

Otto Bettmann, BETTMANN ARCHIVE

You have to simply have the ability to recognize luck, to recognize when there's a chance to move in.

Mary Boone, ART DEALER

I tend to look at things like they happen when they're supposed to. A lot of things happen because they're supposed to happen.

Hal David, SONGWRITER

I believe in luck. I think you make your own, but it's there, whatever it is. I don't think that's a conflict, about making your own. Certain things happen, and that's luck. Some people know what to do with it, some people don't. The chance is missed, and they may not even know the chance is there.

Jeffrey Feinman, PROMOTIONAL CONSULTANT

Luck does play a part. It's a combination of two things: You do everything you can and then it turns out the way it's going to turn out. There are always a thousand things you can't foresee but you don't let that run you.

Mary Boone, ART DEALER

You can't confine success to a single most important factor. On one day I would say one thing. Today I would say *patience*. It hasn't been a bad day at all, but it's been a day when I really understand that there are times to say things and push and there are times to not say things and sit back. Patience is a very important thing. I didn't have as much patience when I began as I have now, and hopefully I don't have as much now as I'll have ten years from now. Patience is something that has to be developed. I think there's not a person in the world who, if you say, "Do you want it now or do you want it later?" will say they want it later.

Jeffrey Hollender, NETWORK FOR LEARNING

I'm a very impatient person. I'm a perfectionist on the one hand, but I'm not the kind of person who likes to do something over and over and over again till I get it right. If I can't get it right immediately and get results, I usually move on to something else or give it to someone else to do.

Jan Stuart, SKIN-CARE PRODUCTS FOR MEN

My father was a businessman who went in and out of businesses. He went bankrupt a couple of times.

My father always wanted a bigger business, always wanted to get involved in different things, never gave it the proper chance, never had the patience to sit down and say, "It's going to take two years for this business to work." Instead, he gave it a year, and if it didn't work in a year he'd go someplace else.

That's why I stuck this out, feeling that anything that's good takes time. It takes time to build a foundation.

We're not talking on the short-term. I can make a lot of money quick, but there has to be some type of illegal scam involved with that. There's no way of making it overnight and staying and surviving. I can make a lot of money, and I'd like to make a lot of money. I would love to have been able to make a lot of money yesterday. I'm starting to make money now, but there's no easy way of doing it.

Jerry Rubin, BUSINESS NETWORKING SALONS

It's All Experience

In the early seventies I was depressed. Then I used yoga, and the attitude that it doesn't make any difference because it's all experience. Obviously there are good experiences and bad experiences; it's good to get your head in a place where you say, Hey, c'mon, it's all experience, so what's the difference?

I'm a survivor. A lot of people from the sixties kind of got stuck and rotated on their own obsessions, and it got to be a problem. I said, If you're a revolutionary, you've got to be a successful revolutionary—what's this thing about martyrdom, where's that at? I met so many people who were self-righteous in their ideas but self-destructive in their behavior; so I say they don't really care enough about their ideas to think about their behavior so that they can be successful in planting their ideas.

I'm just realizing that every day you get hit, and the successful people are the people who keep coming up for the next round.

David Brown, FILM PRODUCER

Stick-to-itiveness

We are working on movie projects, some of which are more than ten years in the making. It takes a great deal of patience and longevity to be a producer.

Life itself is the longest project of all, if you're lucky. And if you do have a goal, such as to be an actress or a composer or a surgeon, then it is very much a matter of stick-to-itiveness. You may have to drop out of school for a couple of years to work, you may have no luck in your profession for a while, but you keep moving, you press on.

You're always having doubts, there's always doubt. Out of perversity, I've persevered. I live on the mistakes of others. I say, Those jerks turned down *E.T.*, what do they know?

It's kind of intuitive wisdom, in reflection, but at the time it's perseverance. It's getting the picture made. When you're out making a movie, as Truffaut said, your main objective is to finish it. That's all you think about. Get finished with the shooting, which is only a minor part of the manufacture of a movie itself.

Jaws was a film we never expected to finish and thought instead might finish our careers. I thought there was potential there for a very good commercial film, but a more careful examination of the production requirements, including that of having a man swallowed by a shark that leaped up on the stern of a boat, might have deterred us from pursuing it because we might have asked the question we later had to ask the production people: "How do we make this movie?" They didn't know. It took a lot of research to find somebody who could do it.

In production, which was hastened by the threat of an actors' strike, we were ill prepared to go to Martha's Vineyard. We had a mechanical shark, but the long journey from the San Fernando Valley to the Atlantic Coast had caused certain ailments in the shark; the saltwater content reversed the polarity of its electrical apparatus, so it had to be changed to a hydraulic system. The result was the shark simply didn't work and Steven Spielberg had to make do with barrels. In the original scene in *Jaws* where a swimmer is swimming around and is brought down, there is no shark. There *was* no shark. There are barrels.

It became so tough; we were there every minute. At one point, Dick Zanuck and I were approached by our production people on the picture and the suggestion was made that we declare a hiatus on the production. This is where experience counts. Dick and I are such combat veterans in movies that we know you don't stop shooting until they take the film out of the camera. So we said, "We don't think you're going to be any better in September than you are in May. Let's keep shooting. Let's never stop shooting, because if we stop we may never start again."

So we were thinking, How do we make this movie work? That's all we were thinking and every day there was a crisis. Our decision was to press onward. That was the major important decision of the movie.

Richard LaMotta, CHIPWICH

People say, "What's the secret to success?" And I have to tell them that it's really perseverance. You don't come along with an idea—there are a lot of great ideas out there—and then sort of sit on the curb and wait for someone to come along and say, "Great idea! Here's a million dollars!" It just doesn't happen that way. Contrary to what a lot of people say, it's never luck. It wasn't luck for the Apple Computer guys, or the guys that strike it rich in an oil well.

Jeffrey Feinman, PROMOTIONAL CONSULTANT

Excess Is Not Enough

I don't perceive us as being creative. We have a formula, we know what works, we apply that formula to a lot of places. When entrepreneurs stop doing one thing, or they sell out to Gulf & Western, they tend to go and do it again in something else. The characteristic of entrepreneurs is they play to win in whatever they do. Watch them play Monopoly some evening. My motto has always been "Excess is not enough."

Failure vs. Temporary Defeat

The only thing I'm clear on that differentiates successful people from unsuccessful people is that successful people recognize the difference between failure and temporary defeat. We've had our share of trouble, but there's a keeping it in perspective. There's another day tomorrow.

The guy who handles our insurance was all excited one day. I asked him if he'd sold somebody on the phone, and he said he'd just gotten turned down. I asked what he was excited about then. He said one out of every ten buys; if someone says "No," he was that much closer to a "Yes." If you can really build that into your head, you're terrific.

David Brown, FILM PRODUCER

Looking Ahead to the Next Project

The movie business is a very forgiving business. Everybody thinks that the next one may be a hit if they don't do business with you, and that is often the case. Even after *1941*, Steven Spielberg kept things going. He had his ideas for future pictures, at all times. It was right after *1941* that he and Lucas concocted *Raiders of the Lost Ark*.

That's the whole point. Always be working on your next project. Don't wait around for your current one to unfold so that you can take a lot of bows. There may be no bows and you'll be damned glad you have something else coming down the road. *Always* be working on something else and don't be dependent on one project. I'm working on four projects now.

As for the reaction to disaster, it's like a death in the family. You wake up in the morning and you think, "Oh, my God, I've got this disaster." You don't hide or anything like that, but it's grief. You have a feeling of grief and you live with it, for a week, a month, a year, and pretty soon you wake up one day and you aren't thinking about it anymore.

CHALLENGE AND RISK

Richard LaMotta, CHIPWICH

No Prisoners

Being an entrepreneur really means putting everything you have on the line, including your reputation, which is most important. I took every dime I had and put it into Chipwich.

When the banker says, "Well, sure, I'll loan you money, you've got a good job and you look like you have the means to pay us back. You own a home. Are you willing to sign personally?" it sounds very innocent. When you sign personally, everything goes—the wife, the kids, the dog, the watch—they leave you with one suit of clothes. That's scary. There's everything you've worked for over a number of years, and it's up on the line. But you have to do that.

Nolan Bushnell, ATARI

Risks

I'm a pragmatic man, with a flair for whimsy. I believe that every one of my decisions is pragmatic. There are a lot of people who perceive me as a nut. But in the end I want to be known as crazy like a fox.

The secret is in not perceiving a risk when everyone else perceives that there is one. I get into a lot of things that to me are sure things, and that everyone else perceives as crazy. I always try to get into things I perceive as sure things, and the bigger the disparity between the fact that I believe it's a sure thing and everyone else thinks it isn't, the greater the chances are I'm going to have a better chance of success, because I'm not meeting any competition.

We did Atari right in the wake of pocket calculators, CB radio, and Hula hoops, and they said, "Hey, video games are the most foolish of all these. I can understand CB radios, I can understand pocket calculators, I can understand digital watches, but video games are just silly. They're games."

Edward McCabe, ADVERTISING EXECUTIVE

Opportunity Is a Form of Security

I don't see most of the things I do as risks. *Risky,* all the time, but not risks. A good balance between security and opportunity is nice. Opportunity is a form of security. Security, to stay where you are, to have a sinecure, to be a vegetable, a nonperson, with no potential and no excitement in what you do, that's not security, that's nonexistence.

Nolan Bushnell, ATARI

Willing to Be Wrong

The thing about life is that you want to not necessarily be wrong, but be *willing* to be wrong. Just do a lot of things and say, "Hey, OK, it wasn't quite right."

Jeffrey Hollender, NETWORK FOR LEARNING

Mistakes

I make major mistakes every day. When I stop making major mistakes I will stop learning because you've got to take chances and you have to take big chances.

Helen Boehm, BOEHM PORCELAIN

That's the secret of life, always learning, every day adding another page to your history.

David Liederman, DAVID'S COOKIES

What Happens If

Most people who go into these kinds of businesses either make it or don't based on their ability to understand the down side, not the up side. Everybody can dream about how many millions of ice-cream cones they're going to sell, how many millions of pounds of cookies, but most people kid themselves about what happens *if*. They don't protect themselves, and that's when they end up getting hurt.

The Gamble

My down side is very, very short. In the beginning I didn't have two nickels to rub together and I owed over a million dollars, that's a big down side. But so what? Let's say I went bankrupt, what do I owe? I have no assets anyway. I was a good talker, so I could convince them to loan me the money.

But I know my down side. And that's why, for instance, I can't stand to gamble. I hate casino gambling, for the simple reason that, let's say I put a dollar on red, it comes up red. Well, if I win, how come I didn't put a million dollars on red? And if I lose, why am I a shmuck for losing the money on red? I can't win. If I lose, I've lost, and if I win, I didn't win enough. So in business I gamble, but they're all calculated gambles.

There's Nothing Better Than Being Smart

You have to be smart. Most of the people who've gotten anyplace are just basically smart. Whether you're smart in food or smart in brain surgery or smart in the manure business, smart is smart, and there's nothing getting around being smart. In my case, I had to be street smart, and I always was street smart; it's something you can't learn. You have the ability to function in the real world.

This man I know is the largest single tenant in New York City. He has more space on lease than anybody else. He makes over seventy-five million dollars a year. He got where he is by being street smart. Once I went to him and I said, "How come everybody thinks you're a son of a bitch?" He said, "I'll tell you, David. I know more than anybody about my business, which is basically the locating of food-service establishments in New York City. Some company will make a deal. I will know their side of the deal better than they know it. So I will work out a deal that this guy will agree to with his two lawyers, and sign away up and down, wagging his head as fast as he can. Six months later he'll come back and tell me I screwed him. I didn't screw him; we negotiated the deal and he signed it. I just was smarter about what he was doing than he was." Which is really what it comes down to.

Jan Stuart, SKIN-CARE PRODUCTS FOR MEN

Instead of following people around, be a leader. They talk about people who have gotten *B*'s and *C*'s in high school being the ones that make it successfully out in life. The ones that got the *A*'s and the *B*'s are the ones that work for a corporation, for a company. They're your management people, they're your corporate people. Goofing off in school, to me, is a manner of self-expression.

I was always the class clown. And look at the class clowns. They're the ones that have that internal drive to make it in life, to make it on their own and to be achievers in business, to do something.

VIII. THE BOTTOM LINE

The dollars and sense of business as understood by those who learned the hard way and took the occasional shortcut. From advertising to Zen

Success may begin with a brilliant or better idea; it becomes a reality only through the understanding and application of sound—if not established—business principles and sense.

Starting up—financing and organizing and hiring—is only the first obstacle to be overcome. Business is also profits and productivity, pricing and promotion, publicity and public relations. It is constant attention to all these matters. In this chapter our entrepreneurs deal with such concerns, providing answers they uncovered during the course of building businesses.

CAPITALIZATION

Dr. Richard Winter, EXECUTIVE HEALTH EXAMINERS

Selling an Idea

I got money by sitting around people's living rooms and telling them the idea I had.

It wasn't easy. But I finally raised a small amount of money through private investors, and we opened that clinic. It became successful and I eventually bought them all out.

Survival Time

We leased, we purchased, we begged, we borrowed the equipment. We used to sit around and figure out survival time, by dividing the monthly loss into how much money was still in the bank, and I knew how much longer I had to go. Fortunately, in the thirteenth month we started to turn a profit. We probably could have gone about three more months, then I would have had to go out and raise more money.

Jeffrey Hollender, NETWORK FOR LEARNING

The Art of Raising Money

I started the Skills Exchange in Toronto with $3,000, and that business grossed about a quarter of a million dollars in the first year. What I didn't have in capital I put in in sweat and blood. I didn't particularly want to do that again—not that you don't put sweat and blood in whenever you go into business—so I raised a lot of money. I had a lot more money starting in New York.

My capitalization the second time was $60,000. Subsequently, a substantial amount of additional money has been put into the business, but when I started it, it was with $60,000. The money all came from private investors. I've never borrowed money from anybody. The investors own part of the business. That's something that has been greatly to my benefit. I don't have any reluctant feelings about having sold a significant portion of my business to other people, because the people who I sold the business to have benefited me not only by their money but by their help and advice. As it happens, the people who are my shareholders and directors—especially now that the business has evolved and become more sophisticated—have played a greater role in moving the business than I would ever have imagined when I first asked them to invest.

Raising money is almost an art. You have to know how to package your idea, you have to know how to present it, and you have to know how to put your numbers together properly. It also happens that it's just as easy to raise $1 million as it is to raise $60,000. I'm raising $1 million right now and I'm doing it much more quickly and easily than I raised $60,000, just because I have the right people and I know how to do it better.

You can borrow money or you can raise money privately or you can raise money publicly. I'm in a position where someone else is raising the money for me, so I don't have to go through those steps. Once you get yourself to a certain point, you can then say, I've got an idea, and I'll pay you 7 percent or 10 percent to raise the money for the idea. That's a much more pleasant way to raise money. But you have to have someone who believes in you enough to raise the money because they put themselves on the line and say, "I think you should invest in this," to their contacts, their clients and friends. So, if you've been successful enough to be able to impress people like that, then you can raise larger amounts of money.

How Much Is Enough?

Within the first year we were making money on a month-to-month basis. We more than doubled the return on our investment at the end of the second year. I wasn't undercapitalized.

One of the biggest problems, as I'm sure many people involved in small businesses will tell you, is that most businesses don't have enough money. Well, there's a very simple formula that I used to raise money: You look at your cash flow, and you look at the greatest amount of money you'll ever lose, and if you're going to lose $50,000 the first year, and $50,000 the second year, and make $2 million the third year, you need to total that up. That's

$100,000 to lose, and you should at least double that.

When I project numbers, I project them under the worst case. I project what I *know* I can do if everything goes wrong rather than what I *think* I can do if everything goes right, because all you're doing is screwing yourself if you do it the other way. So the Toronto experience was invaluable. I could much more intelligently put the numbers together. I learned a tremendous amount up there and I had the opportunity to make mistakes that didn't cost me as much money as they would have if I had made them later in my life.

Ratio of Assets to Liabilities

You can have $1 million in the bank and if you spend $10,000 and make $9,000, you show a loss, but you don't experience any strain in paying the bills because you have lots of capital. You experience strain in paying your bills when you're counting on the money that's coming in tomorrow to pay bills you owed yesterday. That's when you're straining and living on your cash flow, and no business should ever be doing that. As soon as you get close to paying your bills based upon money you expect to receive and haven't yet earned, I believe that's when you raise more money. You might have $100,000 in the bank and $100,000 in bills. Lots of companies live with $100,000 or $1 million in bills, but when the money you have in the bank—your assets—is no greater than your bills—your liabilities—you've got to get more money.

Richard LaMotta, CHIPWICH

At the Bank

For a while I was very skeptical about this American dream. I had really decided, God, you can't do it without a lot of money.

I had tried to get loans and get little businesses going,

and it was so terribly hard. You go to the bankers and they give you the nonsense, "Well, you know, interest rates are 18 percent. If you were here when it was 16 percent, if you were here when it was 14 percent . . ." If you had gone in at 8 percent, he would have said, "Well, you know, it's too high—if you were here when it was 5 percent, I could've done something."

You can't expect miracles from them. We think of banks as these large, magnanimous things—that they're just going to take any idea and invest in it. They can't. That money they have in there belongs to me and you, and others like us—little people. They're investing, hopefully, in the right things. When they lose money, they can't give out as good an interest rate, etcetera. They all get hurt.

I said, Well, I know what I have to do. I don't want to make that same mistake I did in the last business: go in underfunded. So, I'm going to hock the house, I'm going to put everything on the line, I'm going to borrow a lot of money from the bank. I had a pretty good job, so they would loan me money on that.

I eventually got about two hundred thousand dollars out of the bank. But it was collateralized. It was my house, everything. Then I said, Now that I'm up to here in hock, let me go to my friends and tell them my idea and raise some money. I knew that I had to do it all in the right way, with a prospectus and a lawyer. And I raised money from friends, three hundred thousand dollars, and sold them not percentages, but shares, because I knew I would have to raise more money as time went on.

Going for Broke

The idea counts, too, in raising money, but more important than that, you've got to show them that you are in it up to here, you're completely dedicated. You've got to show them that you've got everything you have at risk, because if I come to you for ten thousand dollars of your hard-earned money, and I convince you to give it to me, you'd say, "Gee, is my money the only money you've got at risk? What have *you* got at risk?" You'd want to know that I've got everything at risk.

Nolan Bushnell, ATARI

Every Entrepreneur Mortgages His House

I was singularly unsuccessful at convincing any of the financial community that Atari was a great idea. Then it was in a black box that I could hook onto your television and say, "See, this is what you do." It was only the earnings of the machines in the bars and restaurants that really turned things around.

I got capital after I really didn't need it. We operated the company for the first three and a half to four years without any capital, just on this hand-to-mouth kind of thing. I'd mortgaged my house. Every entrepreneur always mortgages their house.

We were too busy to take on partners. And at the times when we were having troubles, when I was receptive to that, nobody was there. When we weren't having problems, I didn't need the money. Which was good because it ended up giving me a good opportunity to retain a significant ownership position.

Selling Out: Warner Buys Atari

The company had an opportunity to become huge. In order to become huge, it needed approximately $100 million to $150 million in cash, because the consumer business is a seasonal business that requires tremendous cash flow. It cannot be done on the sell-now-for-cash basis. We were used to running the coin-operated business. In the consumer business, you ship in September, you get paid in February. If you're going to sell $100 million worth of product or $200 million worth of product during the Christmas season, you damn well need $100 million of cash.

The company was perceived to have low market capital—not enough that you could ever raise $100 million. So I had to sell. Or go public. Or grow slowly, perhaps miss out on the market. Then, too, remember, I was a poor guy. All of a sudden I had a chance to put $15 million in my back pocket and walk off. That's kind of exciting. All of a sudden you can buy a house, you can buy groceries, and some of that stuff.

It was partially emotional. There's no question that it was time to lock in a certain amount. There was also an aspect of fatigue involved. I'd been through a lot of hell, been undercapitalized perpetually, and so my personal response was, "Hey, get off the risk," and that felt psychologically good.

I've regretted selling. I think I left a lot of opportunity on the table. With the brilliant illumination of 20/20 hindsight, there was perhaps some way I could have done it. I still think it was the right decision based on what we knew at the time. I think nine out of ten pragmatic men would have made the same decision I made at that point in time.

Jan Stuart, SKIN-CARE PRODUCTS FOR MEN

Financing with Credit

My brother quit his job—he was involved in sales, too—and came with me full time. We were living on twenty, thirty bucks a week, running up eight thousand dollars, ten thousand dollars on three MasterCards, three VISA cards.

We would deposit a check and pray that it was not going to bounce. I would take money out of my personal credit line and put it in the bank. I would finagle. I would do everything I could possibly do to make sure I had enough money to survive.

David Liederman, DAVID'S COOKIES

Working Off the Debt

It took a long time to turn a profit. David's and my restaurant were built together and there was massive debt. It cost over half a million to build those two places. I got the money mostly from the contractors. The plumber lent me money, the carpenter lent me money, the electrician lent me money; even the kitchen guy lent me money. It's called notes. It took a long time to pay that back. That store in a sense does very well, but it doesn't make an enormous amount of money because the debt was so high.

Nolan Bushnell, ATARI

I financed Catalyst Technologies with a checkbook. Somebody had to. You never have *enough*, but hopefully, if everything works out OK, my reward will be in heaven. I underestimated how much capital it would take, but it was because of bad projections rather than bad reality.

Liquidity: The Fight Between Fear and Greed

The turnaround time on investments is always five years, but I was hoping it would be less than five years. And it may be. Remember, liquidity is the fight between fear and greed. Well, my guarantee is that I could sell a significant portion of most of the companies I've invested in for a profit right now, but not for as big a profit as I think I can get next year. So, if fear overwhelmed

me right now, I could get myself out. If greed overwhelmed me, I would haul.

It's guts that makes you decide when to sell. The whole
thing comes down to how smart you are.

KEEPING GOING

Richard LaMotta, CHIPWICH

You're always going to be in debt. When I raise equity to wipe out debt, it's only to get to the next pla-
teau, to go from fifteen million dollars in sales to thirty
million dollars, to get into bigger debt. There's only one
way of growing.

John DePasquale, DIRECT MARKETING

Fiscal Conservatism

I'm a very conservative fiscal manager. I probably
could have built the business faster and bigger had I
gambled a little bit more, and borrowed a little bit more
money and expanded a little sooner. I don't know. My
philosophy was, I only will spend what I have, and not
even all of that. So everything that we were doing, all
the building and everything, was out of self-carrying cash.

That's something that, if I had to do it over again, I'd
do differently. Discipline and a methodical approach to
things have been a guiding part of my life, and I really
didn't take enough risks. The fact that I haven't had to
bury any business is not good. It suggests that I didn't
take enough risks. I'm doing it now, but up until the last
year and a half I hadn't.

David Liederman, DAVID'S COOKIES

Cutting Losses

We've closed down about six of the shops. I have no
problem closing a store down. We had a situation where

we closed down one on one block, moved it around the corner, and it did five times as well. We give it a month. We walk. There's an old saying that goes something like: Your best bad money is your first bad money. In other words, if you're losing money, don't compound the problem. We go someplace else.

Richard LaMotta, CHIPWICH

Other Ways of Getting Money

I sold the vendor carts as a tax shelter and then took the money to buy new equipment. I refinanced at the bank. I went and got an old-line investment-banking firm. They at first thought I was either the biggest con man or the best businessman in the world. That's what they said to me. They started with me almost from day one. I said, I don't want your money now. I want to tell you what I'm going to do. I know you're never going to invest with me. I was realistic. I said, But it's my hope that if I'm successful, and you have a history of being with me through all of the steps, that when I do need some money, you'll be there. And they said, OK.

I didn't go to a high flyer. I went to an old-line firm. So old line, I mean they wouldn't touch anybody in a utility deal, you know? I got them to come in and they watched all the little steps and the marketing technique and the newspaper ads and everything build up, and the name, how it was growing, and when I turned around and I needed a little help, they gave me one hundred thousand dollars.

Tax-Shelter Deal

I went out and I said, A cart has a certain price. I paid *x* amount of money, but I can appreciate that because it's got more of a value. I then sold it to a gentleman and said, Look, only put up one fraction of this, and you take a loan from the bank personally for the remainder

on a three-year loan. Lease it to me. I pay off the loan.
You get the tax and the depreciation, and I use the cart
for three years. I'll then take the cart and give it out or
use it as I need. That's the way I raised a couple of million dollars for all those carts I needed. That worked
spectacularly well.

DOING IT WITHOUT MONEY

Jeffrey Feinman, PROMOTIONAL CONSULTANT

Why You Need All That Money

If I were starting out tomorrow I'd start out with more
money behind me. I would find financing. There's almost a Zen concept, where people can sense when you're
hungry. When I was first starting out, a client asked us
to do a project which was worth about $25,000. I was so
desperate to get business I said we'd do it for $5,000.
He never got back to me. Years later he came back with
another $25,000 project and I didn't want to work for him
and didn't want to do the project, so I said $50,000 and
he said fine.

One of the big detriments I had in the beginning was
being so desperate. It's like my married friends who go
out on dates when they're out of town: They have
one night and everyone in the world can sense that desperation. It can't work for you. Dun & Bradstreet has
figured that 90 percent of new businesses go under because they're undercapitalized, and it's probably true.
Especially when rents are $30 a square foot and secre-
taries make $20,000, just the cost of doing business is
staggering.

Absolutely I would have more money behind me, or
not go into business. I would have been a lot better off
if I'd had a switchboard operator and a secretary and
more lavish quarters and not had to worry so much about

where the money was coming from. You should have enough money to last two years without a sale. I had enough money to last till Tuesday if I ate lightly.

John DePasquale, DIRECT MARKETING

Favored Vendors

I cut special deals with a lot of our vendors, saying, "I will give you all my work, and not get prices all the time. You just take five, ten percent off your bills, give me favored-vendor pricing. You don't have to have any salesmen on the account—that makes it worth it for you."

I also sought out small vendors who were in a similar position. The risk there was, if they went out of business when my job was on the press, I'd be in a lot of trouble. On the other hand, we could work together very capably because we were important to each other; it wasn't some little guy dealing with some giant. He was working twenty hours a day, too, so when I was working they were working. Three A.M. phone calls were not unusual at all.

MAKING A PROFIT

John DePasquale, DIRECT MARKETING

Everything Is a Resource

I knew that catalogue-marketing and mail-order-marketing offers and discounts on pots and pans went out in bank billing statements. Little by little, we started to go to our bank clients and say, Now for you, when we do direct mail, we can do other forms of direct marketing. So we leveraged our client relationships, we leveraged our knowledge. Every conception leverages something else.

Dr. Richard Winter, EXECUTIVE HEALTH EXAMINERS

What Else Could We Do?

Once we got organized, the idea was, What else could we do? I remember one of the first sales I made was to Howard Johnson. He'd come in for a checkup, and I knew he was running a little health unit of his own out at his meat-cutting plant on Long Island, and I said, "Howard, I'm going to make a deal with you. I'm not going to sell ice cream, and you should get out of the health business." He said, "You've got a deal." Just like that. So we took over their unit, and there was no financing involved in that because it's in-plant, on other people's premises.

Selling One Idea Several Ways

We have set up a communications group as a subgroup of the corporation, and now are involved in book publishing, movie production, seminars, stress workshops, and different forms of communication on health subjects. We are coproducing movies to support the stress workshops, and the movies will be used for cable television. Once you got the movie in the can, you look for other ways to peddle it. That's the way the thing grows.

COST EFFECTIVENESS

John DePasquale, DIRECT MARKETING

It's Cheaper to Buy Than to Rent

I began to see the dollar liability of large mailings, and then we began to get a lot more sophisticated at what we were doing. We would do copy tests, package tests, paper tests, postage tests with a cadre of free-lance people, then a cadre of free-lance vendors, one guy doing printing, another guy doing envelopes. It was bananas, because the whole thing had to come together in one place, and if one piece was late, you couldn't insert anything. That was the first major problem when I was out on my own. I said, All right, how do we deal with this one? The only way we're going to be in the direct-mail business as opposed to a subset of direct marketing is if we form our own factory. So I set about writing a plan to vertically integrate little by little and form my own factory—meaning computer, lettershop equipment, printing equipment.

I wouldn't call our "factory" a factory then; I hired my brother-in-law and we bought one piece of lettershop equipment, so a lot of the small mailings we were doing we did on our own. Because the small ones were a pain in the neck to everybody else, we were getting charged a premium price; so we were able to make a good economic switch both in terms of control and cost accounting. The big jobs we still contracted out.

David Liederman, DAVID'S COOKIES

Do It Yourself

My fantasy is: I'd like to make my own boxes, I'd like to grow my own nuts, I'd like to do everything. I definitely would like to get my own cow farm, to make my own butter.

Jeffrey Hollender, NETWORK FOR LEARNING

Rent, Don't Buy

We don't have real estate, buildings, mortgages, and all of this huge overhead that goes along with that. Teachers arrange for their own classroom space or we arrange for it and sublet it to them. We can get a better price for them because we can arrange for a large number of spaces and sublet it to them for a cheaper price than they can get individually, but that is a matter of convenience.

Also we don't have a tenured staff that we have to carry; trends change quickly, people's interests change quickly, and we're not stuck with someone who's teaching something there's no longer any interest in. The teachers make a certain amount per student.

Nolan Bushnell, ATARI

Don't Sell if You Can Lease

We were building the machines ourselves. I remember our first production run was 76 units. How'd we come out at 76 units? That was the absolute maximum amount of money we could put together. We figured out every penny that we had, and the number came out to be 76. Not 75, not 74, but 76. I sold them for cash, and the minute I got the cash I took all the profits and paid for the next production run of 210.

We continued selling them outright. We had to because you didn't get fast enough payback if you just put them on location. It was a cash-flow decision, strictly. I would have leased them if I could have. I priced them as high as I possibly could. The initial units were priced at $1,200, and for volume, they'd get down to $950. This was for a unit that was costing us $250 to put together.

EXPANDING

David Liederman, DAVID'S COOKIES

Selling Your Business

I split my time between producing the product and getting real-estate locations. I spend a lot of my time fighting with landlords, haggling with landlords, negotiating with landlords. You can have brokers, you can have lawyers, but you have to make your deals yourself.

I get about 100 to 150 inquiries a week to open franchises all over the world. I have two women who do nothing but try to deal with that. You could say right now it's an embarrassment of riches. There's too much coming in here. Companies pay millions of dollars to develop potential business owners; here they just float in the door.

Jeffrey Hollender, NETWORK FOR LEARNING

Franchising this business is a complicated thing. You hear good things and bad things about franchises. If you want to look at the percentages and the chances of being successful, if you're a franchise versus going into business for yourself, it's about ninety times better to buy a franchise. But this can be a huge pain for the franchiser. In one case, I'm going to propose that we switch it to a joint venture, rather than a franchise, after spending all the money doing all the contracts. It's just not worth it. In the past three or four years, the regulations have changed to make it very, very difficult for the franchiser, and very advantageous for the franchisee. Until you really look at the regulations, you don't realize how tough it is. Two months ago I would have said we're going to have fifty franchises all over the country, but now I'm not sure they won't be joint ventures and owned and operated by us.

John DePasquale, DIRECT MARKETING

Growth: More Trouble Than It's Worth?

Rapid growth gives us a whole new problem to deal with. As an entrepreneur it's a mistake I made—a very costly mistake almost. I talk about always having an optimistic and a pessimitic plan, a recession plan, if you will. The one strategy I really didn't have was for fast growth. I figured that if I grow fast—gee, I should have that problem. But I did have that problem.

Let me tell you: Managing growth is a more difficult process than managing decline. You don't have nearly as many opportunities, you don't have nearly as much lead time to solve problems. So the managing of growth is an often overlooked and critical problem. Right now we are in the process of trying to manage growth, bringing in new people to manage that growth, and having to drop some of the other people because the skills-set isn't what we need. When a company makes that shift from entrepreneurial to corporate, it's a very sensitive moment.

Back-Door Plan

I have a belief that everything you do should have an optimistic and a pessimistic strategy. I call the pessimistic a "back-door plan." You always have to have a back door just in case one of your plans doesn't work. That's not the time to stand there and decide what you want to do. You'd better be prepared to do it, because days could make a difference. I don't see this as negative; I just see it as a problem called opportunity.

Our back-door plan was based on the fact that a factory was a service we could sell to other direct marketers, i.e., our competitors. It occurred to me that not only could we compete with our competition, but we could also complement and serve our competitors, because nobody really wanted to get into the factory business. Today we're the largest independent direct marketer in the country. We now job out to no one. It's all done in-house.

Being able to supply our services to our competition was an alternative to their seeing us as competition. Some big blow comes and we could always say, "Hey, let's make friends and use our own factory and we don't do the agency work.''

Now we are solid enough after all these years in direct marketing that we're starting to do for ourselves what we do for others. We're now starting to put our own money and ideas against our own concepts. That was the other back door, so that if we get into an economy like this one, we're not totally at the whim of the client. The client balks and says, "We're not going to do the program." OK, but at least if you've got some of your own things, you're a bit more in control of your own destiny.

So, we got into some of our other businesses to give us a bit more control of our own destiny. We have seven such businesses.

Jeffrey Hollender, NETWORK FOR LEARNING

I have at times experienced such growth in the business that I said, "Well, we're growing at a rate of 100 percent per year, so I'm going to do some intelligent long-term planning and do some things now to figure out new systems and arrange for something that's going to happen six months down the line." I will never do that without tremendous caution. It's sort of like spending money that's not really in your pocket yet. I anticipated this huge, continued, endless growth and I decided I was going to spend one quarter million dollars on this huge computer system. I started spending the money on the thing and then between the economy and a whole bunch of other things, the growth slowed down and we didn't even need that computer system, and we'd already spent a lot of money on it.

Containing Growth

I've learned that you don't always want growth. You don't always want to take every opportunity that comes along. My tendency is if someone comes along and says, "Hey, I have a way for us to make money," I'll listen and I'll probably pursue it. At a certain point that really becomes a detrimental thing. I only have so much time and I only have so much energy, and if you look at where we've gotten in three years, and you look at how many businesses we're involved in and how much we're doing, there's no way we can take on any more unless I hire someone to run it so that I don't really have to be involved in it.

Gaining Perspective

I think it's difficult for entrepreneurs to cut their losses because they have such a personal stake and involvement in so many of the things they do. Once you have the personal attachment to something, it makes it more difficult to give up.

The more you can think long term and the more you can think in a bigger picture, the easier that becomes to do. That's difficult for a lot of small businesses; they have trouble thinking five years or even two years away. The problems on a day-to-day basis seem so huge that every two months all my managers go away to the country for two days and just think about more long-term problems. If we didn't go away, we would never do it. You have to habitually force that type of thinking or else it just doesn't happen.

COMPETITION AND PRICING

Richard LaMotta, CHIPWICH

Competition Broadens the Market

The nice thing about competition is that it broadens what they call the market category. For example, Chipwich had the ability to make a, let's say, $100-million business out of itself, making the market aware that there's a new kind of product out. What happened when all of the competitors ran in on me was that the awareness factor, instead of being a $100-million market, went to a $300-million market. Now, the guy with the brand name, the guy that's first and sort of creates the generic—he always captures the big share of the market.

Jeffrey Hollender, NETWORK FOR LEARNING

Making a Niche in the Market

It's difficult for a college or a university to compete with what we're doing, for a variety of reasons. One is that they can't offer a lot of courses we offer simply because their trustees and board wouldn't let them.

Someone might say, "If you see UCLA's got the biggest continuing-education program in the country, why are you thinking of going into Los Angeles to compete with it?" Well, because it's huge and it's a great market and there's no one there who's actually involved on an independent basis who is free to offer whatever they want to offer. I know that UCLA wouldn't, couldn't, and has no desire to offer a lot of the courses we make a lot of money on.

John Diebold, MANAGEMENT CONSULTANT

Pricing for Perceived Value

The professional staff here is quite serious, and any new project has to be something that has enough of the client's dollars at stake to make it worthwhile for the client to retain the firm.

If You Have to Ask How Much . . .

I've always tried to have the highest fees in the business for a purpose, which is, I don't want to be in a situation where they're saying, "Well, we'll have advice from them because it's five dollars rather than from the competitor where it's seven dollars." That's not the way to buy advice; if you get into a bidding match and that sort of thing, the chances are reasonable you'll just be sorry for it in the end. So I tell people at the outset when they ask what is the cost of it: "We're the most expensive there is. You can get lower rates from anybody else."

David Liederman, DAVID'S COOKIES

My problem in my particular product is that I am every month gambling on prices. I buy all my chocolate from Switzerland, with Swiss francs. Lately the dollar has been strong, so I do OK. Six months ago, the dollar wasn't so strong, I wasn't doing so OK. In the course of the year, you try to average out. You're going to win some, you're going to lose some. And it's absolutely nuts-making.

If the dollar went back to where it was six months ago against the Swiss franc, my cost would go up about seventy cents a pound, and that's a substantial increase on the wholesale end, because remember, everybody's looking at double or triple retail.

Playing a Volume Game

When I first started out, I looked at how much everything cost me. I looked at how much I thought I had to charge just to make a living and not get rich, under the theory that it's a volume game: I'm not in the precious end of the cookie business. And the number came up at five dollars a pound. So that's where I started. Then various things like butter and chocolate and everything else started increasing. I crept up, both because I had to creep up and also because I wanted to stay ahead of the pack. Now I'm right in the middle of the pack. The other guys are making more money per pound, but I sell many more pounds, so I do better in the long run.

What's going on is an education. People are prepared to spend a disproportionate amount of their income—disposable income or nondisposable income—for food that is better, as long as they don't feel they're getting ripped off. The whole value-for-money thing plays in here.

In this market, there are a number of bakeries where butter cookies are ten, eleven dollars a pound. So when I opened up I was five dollars a pound, and I figured, Well, I guess if I'm selling a cookie that's made with all butter, except it has chocolate in it, which is three times as much as butter, then I'll be positioned pretty well because people will say, "How can you sell a cookie for five dollars a pound which has a lot of chocolate in it, when they're selling it for ten dollars and it's the same butter?"

The other concern was I wanted to be at least a buck more than everybody else. I wanted people to reach a little bit. Not a lot, but a little, to buy the cookies. I wanted to put myself above everybody else. And then everybody creeped up on me and are more expensive now. But I don't feel that the market can take much more than $5.95.

Mary Boone, ART DEALER

I'm a conservative person. The whole thing now is not selling the paintings but keeping the prices down. I think it's very foolish to exploit the market to its highest point, which is very much of a temptation: I know a lot of galleries have done it because when things are selling well you can just keep raising the prices. We raise the prices about 20 percent a show even for artists who have five hundred people for five paintings.

I still think it's important not to act like an auction house, not to put the highest price someone would pay on it, but rather, put a fair price on it so that the next year and the following year and every subsequent year, the artist is selling for more. Also, it means that the secondary market is much stronger. The secondary market is what paintings go for when they are resold. Because if you're selling paintings for absolutely their peak amount, there is no way the secondary market is going to be selling them for more than that, just by definition. I have always maintained that you should underprice the market.

MARKETING, PROMOTION, PUBLICITY, ADVERTISING

David Liederman, DAVID'S COOKIES

Market Research Is a Dirty Word

I don't do any market research. None. It's just my observation. When you're in a small business like mine, market research is a dirty word. You just don't even deal with it. I could commission a study to tell me who eats cookies, for a couple of hundred thousand bucks. For a couple hundred thousand bucks, I could open up four or five cookie stores and if they didn't work I could move them. That's my market research. I firmly believe in that. I'll close down stores, I'll close down businesses, but in the long run I come out ahead.

George Lang, RESTAURATEUR

What I read ranges from the latest in city planning to futurology to a book on packaging to philosophy to sociology to a variety of semi–pseudo-sciences to statistics on what's happening in our business. And then with all that you stick your forefinger in your mouth and you put it up like the ancient sailors used to do to find out which way the wind came from and you try to guess.

It would be really easy for me to give a slick answer on what the common denominator is in marketing in various fields—that you do your market research, you find out what is going to be your market, whether it's china design or a shopping center, a hot-dog stand or whatever, and then you find out likes, dislikes, habits of that particular market and you match it. Thanks a lot. I think the common denominator maybe—*maybe*—is knowing how far is far. How far should you go to give them what they are familiar with and comfortable with and like, and at the same time still feel that they are getting something different, special, and maybe to a small degree adventurous. Maybe that's the common denominator.

Nolan Bushnell, ATARI

Research Doesn't Cover Any Bets

I always ask myself a question: "If this report comes back negative, am I going to abandon the project?" And if the anser is "No," I say, "Why do the report?" I say, "I believe in this product. I know that the world doesn't know what the hell I'm talking about right now, but they'll buy it." You have to be a prophet of sorts.

Helen Boehn, BOEHM PORCELAIN

Whose Idea Is It?

In the marketplace today, everything is being polled— they take the heart out of it. I think when you want to do something, have a lot of faith in yourself. All of these marketing trials and tests take the beauty out of creativity. I love to do something and then just present it. It's my idea. If you're the artist, why do you go out and ask fifteen or twenty people, "Do you like this? Do you like that?" Did Michelangelo do that? Or Raphael? da Vinci? They were commissioned, but they weren't told how to do it.

Richard LaMotta, CHIPWICH

People Are People When It Comes to Ice Cream

I was getting a little worried knowing that Chipwich was a first in a category. Someone else could come along and jump on that, and I could be out. I knew in my gut I had a good product. I didn't need ten million dollars' worth of group testing. The people in New Jersey are no different from the people in Ohio, nor different from anybody in California, when it comes to ice cream and good quality; and I had raves. And I said, Wow, people really love this.

I have six hundred streetcarts now. I have a network. Matter of fact, I have probably the most successful test marketing and sales network in the United States. Our six hundred vendors are equivalent to a compnay the size of Kraft, doing over twelve billion dollars a year with six hundred salesmen. We have six hundred active salesmen and people are seeing the name all over those little billboards.

Jan Stuart, SKIN-CARE PRODUCTS FOR MEN

Customized Marketing

To save money, I lived at the Ninety-second Street Y—after living in a nice apartment in New York.

I was paying forty bucks a week living at the Y. Everything has its place and there's a reason for everything. There were four hundred people at the Y. And to do a marketing program of the products would have cost a fortune. I ran into a guy the other day who said he would do a marketing program, for ten thousand dollars would give one hundred people our product to try. I had four hundred people in the Ninety-second Street Y who shaved every day. I had a built-in clientele. We were giving samples to all the people in the Y and had a bulletin board in there saying, TELL ME HOW YOU LIKE IT. These people were getting free samples, they were getting free shaving cream. They loved it. So it was a great marketing program. I didn't know anything about marketing at all.

Richard LaMotta, CHIPWICH

A New Market Category

I think Chipwich, Inc. is an image, and the image that Chipwich built was one of quality. There is no category of premium novelty: We're going to be it. We can charge a dollar because people are going to pick up a treat, and people are going to say, "Yeah, well, it's about time. They've been feeding me this garbage for fifty-five cents that has no vanilla in it, no chocolate, no real ice cream." There's a market for people who want to treat themselves to the best.

Jan Stuart, SKIN-CARE PRODUCTS FOR MEN

A Niche in the Market

The reason I went into the men's skin-care area is I found a niche in the market. Being a designer or going into a woman's line like Estée Lauder, the competition was too vast: You need so many dollars for advertising. But getting involved in the men's market—it was a new market and nobody was doing it at all, so with very little money I was able to make my name in the market, and all it called for was basic education and push.

Pinpointing Markets

I figured, men's cosmetics, men's skin care: automatic sales to the gay market. But the gay market was new to me. Here I am, this straight kid from New York going into the gay market. How did I find out about the gay market? I started buying gay magazines and finding out who the publishers were and calling them up and talking to them about how I wanted to take my skin-care products and put them in their magazines. I started doing mail order out of all the gay magazines.

The response wasn't super as far as mail order, but I got a lot of exposure. The department-store people were all reading my ads and calling me up and I was getting some nice responses.

I felt that I couldn't really sell the stores. I had to prove myself. I had to do something. I figured my next venture was the bathhouses. So Jan Stuart went catering his wares to all the gay bathhouses, carrying boxes of products to all these guys wearing towels. I didn't know anything about the gay market, was totally inhibited giving demonstrations. We started selling to the gay market, and started doing well. I was selling out of shopping bags.

Then I heard the story about how Mary Kay was doing so well. I said, "If Mary Kay can do it, why can't I?" That's when I decided to start doing a Mary Kay for the gay market. I started advertising in *The Village Voice*.

This is how we got our exposure. And the sales started coming. Our name started getting around.

Richard Winter, EXECUTIVE HEALTH EXAMINERS

Creating a Perceived Need

I was looking for a reason: Why an executive-health library, what's different about executives? So I decided,

I'm going to create a new branch of medicine; it's going to be called *executive health,* like geriatrics or whatever. Why not?

So then I thought to myself, What's the justification for creating this new branch of health? An executive is exposed to things that other people are exposed to. He has to make decisions with inadequate information, and that's stressful. He has to travel constantly, he has to eat meals in restaurants, he has to work long hours, he has to do this and that. So I said, Well, a painter has to work long hours, too, but only in the executive are all of these things embodied in one person. A painter doesn't have the stress of decision making, unless the stress is deciding whether the pink he's painting the walls should have a little more pink. For the executive we're talking about serious things, where great sums of money or the lives of people are involved, and he has to do this combined with long working hours, travel, all this. Only in the executive do all these factors come to play simultaneously, so that makes him a special person with special problems. Example: It's a lot easier to be on a diet if you're eating at home than if you have to eat in restaurants all the time. The *Executive Health* books were written with that theory in mind. So if you want to go to a restaurant and have a drink, have a spritzer; that's only ninety calories, as opposed to a martini.

The other thing is, what we're trying to do with these books and other things is really say that an examination is just one step in a total health experience. What we're trying to create is a total health experience for people. We're also trying to create a perceived need for that.

Jeffrey Hollender, NETWORK FOR LEARNING

An Intelligent Marketing Device

My father was the head of Grey International Advertising, and I credit him with being a great businessman and a great help to me in my advertising and my marketing.

When I was a little kid, Grey always had to decide which of the new cartoons and children's shows they were going to put their clients' ads on, and so for weeks and weeks people would be coming in and showing their programs. His solution was always to bring me and my brother in and sit us down and let us watch hours and hours of cartoons. We loved it. Whatever we liked was usually what they would buy because he figured there was no better way he could figure out what children were going to like than having children decide. That is an intelligent marketing device.

The fact that most of my clientele is female means that, first of all, if I ever have just men working around me I know I'm in trouble, because I can't adopt that point of view.

Lois Wyse, ADVERTISING EXECUTIVE

Playing Up Your Advantages

Being a woman has only been an advantage, an enormous advantage in every way. People are less suspicious of women. Men respond very well to women. I don't know if they took me seriously, but I sold a lot. Men really try to help you. Men have been marvelous to me in business, really taught me a lot. I'm not sure they would have been as patient and understanding with another man as they were with me because they would have expected more of him. When I was young, men had no expectations with regard to women, so that anything I could do, it was "Ah! How amazing! She can walk across the room without falling down! Isn't that nice!"

Now it's an enormous advantage to be a woman because so much of my business is communicating with what women are today, and advertisers are perfectly willing to believe that I know an enormous amount about it because I'm one of them. Now I'm where the action is; I'm a woman who works and is "successful"—whatever that means. But I'm a woman who works and who runs a business and so I'm doing what they think women want to do. What they don't realize is that many women, as soon as they can, run to get out, get married and have children.

Jan Stuart, SKIN-CARE PRODUCTS FOR MEN

Mail-Order Advertising

I was fortunate enough to hook up with an art director who helped me do the packaging. He put together my first ad. I couldn't afford to do straight advertising; it cost too much. I figured if I incorporated mail order with advertising, I would be able to do mail order, which I heard was a tremendous amount of business. And mail order would give me the exposure before capturing the retail market.

Agency Discount

In advertising, if you start your own agency you get your own discount and save 15 percent. So I had my own ad agency to insert my mail orders. Being an agency, I was able to delay payment of my ads for 90, 120 days. So I was able to keep on running my ads. It was like a credit card.

Jerry Rubin, BUSINESS NETWORKING SALONS

Publicity: Generating Interest

I don't seek publicity. It comes to me. I believe the best publicity person is someone who makes news and then gets people interested.

Jeffrey Hollender, NETWORK FOR LEARNING

Generating Publicity

Lots of times we create courses simply because we can generate a lot of publicity—whether or not anyone ever registers for the course is of secondary interest. Like "The Art of Social Climbing," or "How to Marry Money," which were created as vehicles to get publicity. The "How to Marry Money" teacher, Joanna Steichen, photographer Edward Steichen's widow, was on *Good Morning America, The Today Show,* and *Donahue.* That course happened to attract a lot of students as well as generating a tremendous amount of publicity, which in turn benefited all the other courses.

If you want to do something on a national basis, you have to prove that you have national appeal, and one of the ways you prove that is by generating national publicity. If Indiana radio stations want to interview you on your course, that's something you can sell to Warner Amex or any national company that's going to distribute and sell what you have nationally. It's a big jump to be able to go from being a local business creating, producing, and packaging things in New York to a national business. There's no replacement for the publicity we got.

David Liederman, DAVID'S COOKIES

The success of David's Cookies has a lot to do with quality. It also has a lot to do with my personal ability to get mostly good publicity. I learned how to give good interviews. I learned that you can't bullshit reporters, you just have to say what you really feel, and some things are going to make you sound like an idiot but some things are going to ring true. I've had my run-ins with the various powers of the food press, but I think they respect me because if they write something I don't agree with, I'll call them up and tell them.

Richard LaMotta, CHIPWICH

I hired a man to help me run marketing and he said "We need three million dollars for advertising." I said, "I don't have three million dollars in the whole company. I'm going to go out and I'm going to go to Albuquerque, New Mexico, and to New Orleans, and to Texas." And he said, "You can't do all of that." And I said, "Watch. I'm going to spend five months on the road and I'm going to be in every radio, TV, and newspaper, and I'm going to tell them the story of Chipwich."

There were 278 major stories on Chipwich.

Wally "Famous" Amos

I was promoting all along. I never stopped promoting for one second. I had birthday parties. We had a band, gave away thousands of cookies, and milk and champagne. In Honolulu, I did a big promotion. I called it the "cookielau." They have what is called a *hukilau* in Honolulu, and when I moved there I made it *cookielau*, which is a natural. We'd take over a big park and have local entertainers, groups and singers, and we'd hook up with a dairy and they'd give milk and dairy products and I supplied the cookies. We'd have parachuters come into the park, and it was just incredible. People would just come and spread out their blankets and make a day of it.

I had a promotion once in Tucson, Arizona, when I started selling cookies in a department store there. I decided that I wanted to land at the mall in a helicopter, and I called the helicopter "Cookie One"; the whole thing was a takeoff on the President and his plane, Air Force One. We rented this helicopter and I landed, and when I arrived I had a kazoo band that met me when I came off the plane and I had the cookie on a satin pillow. The cookie was the guest of honor.

We're promoting fun, the fact that the cookie makes you feel good. I gave the cookie a personality. I made this cookie really happy, energetic, friendly.

It was a show-business concept: I managed the cookie. In the press kit, there's an eight-by-ten glossy of the cookie. It's a star; it's got to have a press kit.

I'd been in show business for fourteen years, so all I did was transfer this concept to the cookie. Having that concept, it could be anything I wanted it to be. I always see it as a comedy—it's not a rock act, it's not a Shakespearean actor, it's a comedy. The first commercial I did, I pretended the cookie was opening in Las Vegas, and made this big fanfare: "Ladies and gentlemen, the Famous Amos Chocolate-Chip Cookie Society proudly presents the delicious, the delectable, the Famous Amos Chocolate-Chip Cookie!" It's all show business; given that concept, you could do all those silly things.

Richard LaMotta, CHIPWICH

I have a thousand carts. A thousand carts selling two hundred Chipwiches a day. That's two hundred thousand sales in a day. How many times does that kid say the word "Chipwich"? How many people are passing a Chipwich cart a day? Hundreds of thousands. How many impressions does Chipwich make with a thousand carts out there, owned and operated and done our way?

In the metropolitan areas, which are the real buying areas right now, all these people don't live here. They go home and say to their family, "I had this great product. I hear it's being sold in some markets. Let's go out and buy some Chipwiches." It's like you saying to a friend, "Did you taste Häagen-Dazs's new maple-walnut?" And your friend runs out one day, and she remembers that you said maple-walnut. I could not have planned it any better. It was just perfect.

Helen Boehm, BOEHM PORCELAIN

My beat is really all over the world.

The first big break was in 1951. The Metropolitan Museum put two of my husband's early pieces in its collection. First I'd started showing his porcelain to the stores, the lovely galleries in New York. But they'd never heard of Boehm, and said it would take a hundred years. So I knew I had to take a shortcut—because the quality was there, the good sculpture. But how did you convince Tiffany? So I thought, Let me try first getting it into the Museum, and I was very fortunate because they said it was superb work. I had to do it that way; when they told me it was going to take me fifty to a hundred years, I said, Let me be recognized by those in the field, the scholars—which meant the museum. Then, when I made the Metropolitan Museum, I was able to go back to those people at the stores and say, "Listen, his work is in the Metropolitan." Suddenly there was a stamp of approval, and they started buying one or two birds, one or two horses. It was still quite an uphill battle. We started in a few stores in New York, and then we branched out a little bit in Boston and Philadelphia. I'd come home to New Jersey at night so I wouldn't have to stay in a hotel; I couldn't afford to.

We had a beautiful, whimsical break: I was having a

show at Tiffany, and my husband had beautiful live birds from all over the world. He loaned me some for the show at Tiffany, and as I was unloading the birds in front of Tiffany, they all escaped; it made six hundred papers throughout the world. I can't repeat what my husband said.

Timely Connections

Current events are very important; sometimes you can design artistic things with a timely connection. My feeling for marketing has always been that you've got to do everything big, but you've got to do everything with sincerity. Sure, there has to be a marketing aspect, but the idea must be something that is natural, and my presenting President Eisenhower with porcelain Hereford bulls just after he'd gone into beef cattle was. When the Metropolitan bought the first pieces, I wrote to Mrs. Eisenhower and told her I was the wife of the only porcelain maker who'd made the Met, and I'd like so much to present her with one of the Hereford bulls. So that was marketing, and I knew we'd be in two famous places, the White House and the Met. We've served eight Presidents.

I had known that President Nixon was going to China and I wrote him that we were making life-size procelain swans. Just about a month before he went to China, he called and said, "How about a gift for the Chairman?" He had always taken Boehm birds to NATO countries.

Otto Bettmann,   BETTMANN ARCHIVE

I'd built up my archive enormously, and I must admit I had a certain sense of merchandising and promotion. I had a great, seemingly hidden talent for expanding not only my archive but my hold on the marketplace.

I had printed little catalogues. I looked out for special

occasions, be they anniversaries or new discoveries. If there was a new aviation trend it was quite natural that I would move in with subject matter. Perspective is really one of our greatest shortages and there's always this craving for seeing how it all came about. In a factory where people grouse and cry and complain, show them sometime a picture of how factories were in the so-called good old days. There's always a certain uplift with the idea that things are better now.

New developments came up—let's say computers—and naturally I followed this up. We would then send a little sheet with pictures of early computers and show the primitive things. Or new energy sources. Atomic energy, how did it all come about?

The Business of Putting Things in Perspective

Take the fear of destruction. Is that really something new that we all fear—destruction, that this is the end of the world? The heavens will fall down and we will all be destroyed? This is a fear that reaches back eons; when Prometheus brought fire down from heaven, everyone thought the whole world would go up in flames. We always had this enormous fear. When you had the Three Mile Island scare—it goes back to the Bible, where God threatens the world with destruction. All these themes come up out of the ocean of history.

We had a pretty good selection on this subject. These I would send to firms. I looked in the advertising register and sent them out to energy companies, to light and power companies and other things. But then we also sit and wait until editors come to us. At this point, it has really grown to such a degree that not terribly much is done these days in the Bettmann Archive in terms of active promotion.

You get a certain feeling. Maybe I had a certain sensitivity to needs. It's come rather naturally; it's something you must develop.

IX. THE HEART OF THE MATTER

Running a business is ultimately an exercise in dealing with people

THE PERSONAL TOUCH

Jeffrey Feinman, PROMOTIONAL CONSULTANT

Sacrifices Required by Growth

Unfortunately, some of the clients you really like can't afford the price you now command and, too, you can't service all the business yourself. Just as if you look up from the operating table and instead of Dr. X, whom you're paying for, there's a resident operating on you, business clients frequently resent the fact that it's a production manager going with them to a press conference. Even though the production manager may know more about it than I do, they've lost the pressing the flesh and that personal-service aspect. So, with a lot of the business I got because it was me and they liked me, I now have the other problem, which is that there's only a finite number of hours in the day and I have to turn business over to somebody else; clients don't like the somebody-else idea.

Jan Stuart, SKIN-CARE PRODUCTS FOR MEN

You Are the Company

The thing I had going for me was that there was a Jan Stuart, and Jan Stuart was in the store all the time, bringing a lot of excitement and selling his products.

Norma Kamali, FASHION DESIGNER

You Are the Business

When I opened O.M.O. (On My Own) about five years ago, Geraldine Stutz [president of Henri Bendel department store] was very helpful and spent a lot of time with me. In her experience as the head of a company, she had found that it was very important that no matter what problems or troubles she was having, she had to hide them from everyone else and keep a smile on her face and a good attitude, because the energy of the store, the energy of the people around her, would change with her mood changes. It was very important that she keep their energy up and solve the problems by herself so that the whole store wouldn't feel the gloom of the problem.

That is absolutely the truth. I find that when I *don't* listen to that advice and go ahead and tell my feelings, it doesn't work. Because people feel the tragedy with you, the whole company goes into a severe gloom and nothing is worse than having everybody in a bad mood or feeling terrible. If anybody walked into the shop or office, they'd ask, "What is going on here?" But the energy I put out is contagious also—so whatever *you* are feeling, your people are going to feel.

Jan Stuart, SKIN-CARE PRODUCTS FOR MEN

Independence Carries a Price: Responsibility

After a while, you feel like you're a fireman with a red hat: All you do is have little fires. That's what it is to own your own business.

Otto Bettmann, BETTMANN ARCHIVE

The business is out of my hands pretty much. This in itself is rather a point of pride to me, that this was not a personal business but one that I could transfer and one that still runs in its merry way.

Jeffrey Hollender, NETWORK FOR LEARNING

Delegating Responsibility

I think it's a real mistake not to delegate responsibility. The type of thing that entrepreneurs don't like to give up is the press, for example. They want to be in the spotlight when an interview comes. There's going to be a day when an important interview comes around and I'm not going to be able to do it. If I don't let others do the interviews, and let them learn how to do them well, then in the long range I'm doing something that's detrimental to my business because I need someone else who can do that. It's not something I ever want to become uninvolved in, because public relations and the image that your business has is a very important thing. It's very important how people perceive the character of the business, the way we do business, our integrity, all those things. I obviously want to keep close control over that, but at the same time it's important to let other people around here share the spotlight with me.

I try to give people as much responsibility as they're capable of handling. Whenever you give someone a job, unless you give them enough real authority to go along with it and real responsibility, I don't think they'll ever be able to do a good job.

I had someone in Houston who was running the Network for Learning program there, and now she's going to run the program in New York. I was saying to her how important it was that she take the program on as if it were her own thing, and she take the care that I had when I started, because it needs that. It's a living thing. Now, if I tell her that and at the same time tie her hands behind her back, so that if she wants to spend money she can't, if she wants to fire someone she can't, then she can't do it. She won't have the opportunity to make it her own project.

Ultimately, giving people a percentage of the business is an important thing to do. I do that cautiously and carefully because this is a young company and I don't go throwing away chunks of it. But I believe people should participate in a way that is greater than just their salary.

One of the exciting things is when you have one person running one division and another person running another division; it's exciting because they're both trying to do the most with their project.

Jerry Rubin, BUSINESS NETWORKING SALONS

Rewards for Results

I believe in small rewards for good results. But I know it opens up a Pandora's box. You always ask for more when you're given a little. It's an old counterrevolutionary principle: Give people a little and they start biting off your hand.

Christopher Whittle, CHAIRMAN, *ESQUIRE* MAGAZINE

The Pie Will Get Bigger

Sharing rewards increases your own. If people don't feel like they are part—and, in fact, are not part—then why should they care? If you're going to be in business, which is by definition a team effort, I think sharing rewards is crucial and will ultimately contribute to your own success.

We have always believed in the concept of "It's OK to slice the pie because it'll get bigger," and have been, I think, in the forefront of sharing with people in the company who are really contributing to its success. I don't mean just equity but also immediate rewards. There are all sorts of forms that that takes, from salary to performance incentives to stock to whatever. But it is a sharing: I definitely have seen people that don't do it, and I think it holds them back. I think that they pay for it, and they are less successful because they in fact keep their people from being successful. They don't give them the rewards and the incentive; therefore, the people don't care. Why should they die over little items when they can't see why? I know what's contributed to my success is that we have an extremely talented group of people in the company, and we've really gone out of our way to try to make those people a part of it.

Jeffrey Hollender, NETWORK FOR LEARNING

Appreciating Everybody's Interest

I want my instructors to make as much money as possible. They are paid on a per-student basis. They are my greatest asset in a sense, and therefore I don't offer courses that compete with each other. I won't add a whole bunch of courses if I think I'm going to do nothing but dilute the number of students I have among other courses, because when you're in business, you need to appreciate everybody's concern and everybody's interest.

I work with my printer with the same philosophy that I use with my teachers. For example, I might go down to print the catalogue and the printer might make a mistake. I would be entitled to reprint the whole catalogue. Well, I wouldn't have him do that unless the mistake was very serious, even though I'm entitled to. A lot of people would say, "It isn't right, I want you to do it over," but I know that I get a whole array of benefits because he likes to do business with me. I get my job done more quickly, it gets more attention, his best people get assigned to it—basically because he likes me and he knows that I take his point of view into account as well as my own. If the mistake he's made isn't going to hurt me, then I'll overlook it, because next time I might walk in and he might start printing the job and I might say, "Geez, I changed my mind about something." Now, he could say to me, "Jeff, that's going to cost you for me to change it." But he won't; so it pays off.

You've got to look at everything in the long term.

Wally "Famous" Amos

People Work for Themselves

People don't work for me. They work *with* me; they work for themselves. And they are responsible for doing a good job, and if they live up to their responsibilities, then we'll have a great company and we'll all make money. If they don't, they'll be terminated and we'll find someone else. So I am not responsible for those people; I am responsible for me. I am responsible to the company.

I'm responsible for promoting Famous Amos, and seeing that the working environment and conditions are good, and pleasant, and giving people the opportunity to realize whatever it is they wish to realize.

PERSONNEL

John Diebold, MANAGEMENT CONSULTANT

In the end, running a business is essentially a personnel job. People who serve the personnel function in companies tend to be looked down on, but essentially the top management function is a personnel job. It's a question of selection. You must be very careful and very selective.

There weren't many people in our field. In the beginning it was very tough finding people. The best were really people who were good people and then they gradually learned about the field. I only discovered about hiring very late in the day. It's an obvious fact, but it wasn't obvious to me. I was focusing on all kinds of other things. I would get very influenced by people floating around with super credentials. Much later I realized that only one or two people lived up to the credentials, and I spent more time trying to study the people. It's very tough, I think, because you don't really know how people behave unless you've worked with them for a while. So it's very hard when you're hiring.

Nolan Bushnell, ATARI

Overpromoting

I handled the rapid growth by trying to hire well. Sometimes I didn't. Overpromoting. You take a guy who's doing a really great job as head of a department that's maybe $10 million in sales and he absolutely falls apart at $15 million. The Peter Principle is absolutely true; he's exceeded his capabilities. Maybe if it had taken three years for the company to go from $10 million to $15 million in that particular department, he could have handled it. But he was just sort of hanging on by his fingertips at $10 million.

Lois Wyse, ADVERTISING EXECUTIVE

The Single Hardest Thing

I would probably make all the mistakes again. The biggest mistakes have been mistakes in judgment, which are the biggest mistakes everybody makes. The biggest mistakes I've made have probably been in hiring. That's the single hardest thing to do in business. You make mistakes in hiring, but they don't help you the next time because you'll just go out and make the same mistakes again anyhow.

Edward McCabe, ADVERTISING EXECUTIVE

I've been too hard on people at times and expected too much from them, and expected them to be me because I'm the only one I really know. So I got into sort of thinking that everyone thinks exactly the same way I do, and should see things the way I do. Over the years I've been learning a lot. There are some people I've lost that I wish I hadn't. And we all have people we've not lost but wish we had.

Jeffrey Hollender, NETWORK FOR LEARNING

I've gotten to the point where I can now fire people. I can fire anyone. I don't get all nervous about it, but that took a long time. I'm still not good at hiring people. I still spend too much time telling them why they should work for me, rather than finding out whether or not they're right for us.

Nolan Bushnell, ATARI

Screens

Historical screens pick up historical products, and we want to see the future.

We look for sparkle, dedication, a little greed, a certain amount of larceny. Controllable larceny. Controllable by me.

Whenever you hire someone or bet on someone, you

want their judgment, and judgment is one of those things. It's not intelligence, it's not capability, it's something else. It's judgment. I know it when I see it.

Having been fired from a big company might be a benefit.

John DePasquale, DIRECT MARKETING

I try to hire people based on what the position is. Certain positions require just big thinkers, and any kind of detail that they thought of would just be a waste of time. Other positions require just detail, and some both. More important, however, are trust and honor and integrity.

Helen Boehm, BOEHM PORCELAIN

More businesses fail for lack of knowledge than for lack of money. They fail for lack of knowledge and administration.

Putting the right person in the right position is necessary to protect your reputation, your future. There are certain parts of the business that I think other people can do better than I can, and for me to do them would dilute me on those things I can do better than anyone else. So part of it is figuring out what I'm best at—and what others are best at.

Jeffrey Hollender, NETWORK FOR LEARNING

Overextending Yourself

I have to look at what my contribution is to the business in a realistic sense: how much I can expect other people to do and how much I have to do.

One of the contributions I make that seems to be essential is a creative contribution, and if I spread myself too thin I can't do enough creative work on any of these projects. Whether it's writing an ad or conceptually designing a consulting program, those things take time. I have in many situations got myself where I had nothing but appointments for five days in a row—or six or seven days in a row—and I can't even do any creative work, and it's important for the business that I be able to do that.

I obviously try to hire good people, but there are certain things, no matter how much I turn over to someone else, where sometimes I do have to step in.

PARTNERSHIPS AND COLLABORATION

Christopher Whittle, CHAIRMAN, *ESQUIRE* MAGAZINE

Division of Labor

I have about as much to do with the editorial side as most business heads in magazine situations, which is a relatively minor amount, and it's best that way. It's always been that way. One of the reasons Phillip Moffitt and I have worked together for thirteen years is we've divided things well so that the gray areas are not too many; I generally run the business and he generally runs the editorial. That saves us both a lot of time so that we can do what we do well. It's a good way to run a magazine company because you don't want the businessmen editing the book.

Reducing the Number of Blind Spots

Partnerships is one of the things on my list of things that have helped us succeed. My major collaboration has been with Phillip, and there is no question that the combination of the team is better than the two individuals.

We make better decisions, because all people have blind spots and you just miss things on your own—completely. And when I say collaboration, I mean a collaboration of equals, because a collaboration of equals is different from having a staff: The staff may not be in a position to really stand up against the wall and say, "Hey, look." I think going it with one other person is a wise move.

Good partnerships are very rare, but when they work they're very powerful. First of all, not only do you have blind spots, but you have lapses. You just have periods in your career where you're kind of out of it, and that's not to say that you're completely ineffective. It just means you're not running at peak power. Those times don't necessarily coincide, so that I may be running at 70 percent and Moffitt may be running at 120 percent for a certain stretch, and then that flips around at some other time.

This has enormous advantages. Drawbacks don't really come to mind: There's just one that kind of floats in there. There is always the lingering question, How would you do alone? and I would have to rate that as a potential drawback. I think there are solutions to that problem: doing separate projects and having clear lines of responsibility. Particularly as you grow, there are solutions to that because as the business enlarges its spheres are really very separate, so you get to see how you do alone.

David Brown, FILM PRODUCER

A Partner Is a Wailing Wall

A common history is nice. Dick Zanuck is eighteen years younger than I am. When the studio fell apart we were left in Siberia together and we suffered together. We went through hard times together. Then we became great personal friends; although we have totally antithetical interests and we live on opposite coasts, we're the closest personal friends. That is not always true of partners. We're empathetic, but we're not cronies.

Seeking a partner is seeking a wailing wall, somebody to commiserate with. I don't find anything wrong with having just two people. We have the smallest company in the business in terms of number of persons. We have nine people, including ourselves, on both coasts.

Movies are different from almost every other activity on earth in that they are collaborative to a great extent. What starts as the vision of one or two producers, then adds a screenwriter, then if everything works out, adds a budget department. You certainly have hundreds of people involved throughout the various phases of making a movie. Any one of these groups of people can sink the project.

Hal David, SONGWRITER

There's Got to Be a Chemistry

Teaming up with Burt Bacharach was a lucky turn, but it almost had to happen. Any collaboration in our business is so chancy. You can put two marvelous people together, for example, Alan Lerner and Richard Rodgers, and nothing happens! Or, Stephen Sondheim and Richard Rodgers. Good people, and there are examples ad infinitum like that. So beside bringing two people of good talent together, there's got to be a chemistry. It's very much like two people in any situation—man and woman. What makes it work is that little chemistry that nobody knows about.

At that time in New York, the music business was taking place in two or three buildings. One was the Brill building, which was the Mecca. Everyone knew everyone. In a week's time, you'd run into most of the people in your business. You really had a chance to meet everybody.

There were enormous piano rooms, where the publishers made space available to you to work if they thought you were talented. You were sort of obligated to play your material for them, and so you met everybody, you wrote with everybody. Everyone wrote with everyone—everyone was looking for that magic combination. Everyone still is. I knew everybody's songs; they knew my songs. You sort of rooted for each other, and you wondered at the same time how come they were making it and you were not? And they would probably feel the same way. And at one point, Burt and I were working next door to each other. One day we tried a few songs together, and from that moment on it was terrific.

X. COLLECTED WISDOM

Lessons learned out of school, including some amusing anecdotes and observations about human nature

THE KINDNESS OF STRANGERS

Jeffrey Feinman, PROMOTIONAL CONSULTANT

Your First Kiss

I took this little office space and assumed the business would pour in. For a long time nothing happened. Then a piece of business came in from just a nice guy who's still a client of ours. He was an older guy, and later when I asked him, "Why are you giving me this business?" he said, "Do you remember the first girl you ever kissed?" I said, "Yeah." "Do you remember the third?" I said, "No." He said, "I'll always be your first client." To this day, he can call me at any time day or night and I'll do anything for him.

Lois Wyse, ADVERTISING EXECUTIVE

The Best Way to Make a Friend Is to Ask Him to Do Something for You

The thing that really happened was that people were marvelous to us in the beginning. Most people were very interested in us and they thought of us as kids. We were very young, really *so* young when we started out. I went to work at seventeen. Everybody sort of felt sorry for us and wanted to help us out, they had a lot of feeling for us. People didn't give us accounts as favors; they liked themselves for being able to trust us.

Nobody gives you anything as a favor, but it makes people feel good about themselves because they've been able to do something for you. Somebody told me once that the best way to make a friend is to ask for something that can be given easily. The best way to make a friend is not to ask *for* something, but to ask someone to *do* something for you. That person stays your friend.

In the early days, we asked people to give us an opportunity to handle a small part of their business. We never went asking for the whole thing. We'd ask for a small piece, a little bit of this, a little bit of that.

Richard LaMotta, CHIPWICH

People Want You to Succeed

America wants to hear that the Horatio Alger story is alive and well, and that you don't need special talents. They're buying the product, the story, everything. There's a fanatical loyalty in the United States to that dream. People want to believe it and they support you.

There were nine thousand reasons not to buy the Apple Computer. It was certainly not the only microprocessor in the world. Honeywell had them. IBM had them. Everybody had them. If you're thinking in a logical way as a businessman, you say, What if Apple computer goes out of business? A young guy—he's got nothing to service me. How's it going to be done? But there's that belief, the empathy. So you buy Apple, you support him. People are loyal to it, versus the big guy who'd already made it.

That's the beautiful part about America. People spurred

me on. They wrote me letters: "God bless you. You're doing the right thing. Stay with it. Hang in there."

MAKING CONTACT

Christopher Whittle, CHAIRMAN, *ESQUIRE* MAGAZINE

First Impressions

One thing I try to teach to all of our marketing people when they go out in the world and meet people is truly that your first impression is your last. The greatest impact you'll ever have is that first meeting. You are categorized, pigeonholed, labeled in those moments. It's crucial that those beginning experiences with people, whoever they are, are right. That goes for somebody you're recruiting as well as somebody that you're attempting to sell.

It is those first little moments that determine the rest of your relationship, and that is often forgotten. Great thought and care should go into those beginning things. As an example, I find it true in bringing people into our organization. The setting of the reality begins in the recruiting process, not when they join; the impression has already been made by the time they arrive. So literally, when you're just interviewing them, you have to be sensitive to the fact that *that* point is when they begin to view you—not the day that you're officially their boss.

Jeffrey Feinman, PROMOTIONAL CONSULTANT

Appearances Count

If you're selling General Foods, for all their lip service for wanting to help small entrepreneurial business, you are ultimately not selling General Foods; you're selling a brand manager and a product manager who puts his job on the line every time he makes a purchase. And at some point he has to defend that by answering, "Why are you buying from this guy in a basement in Queens?"

The stuff we can get away with, now that we're successful, we couldn't get away with when we were starting out. Now we can move to Long Island City and be in a loft; now I can wear jeans to the office; now when I go out to eat I can order hamburger instead of steak because I prefer it. Back then, they would have thought I couldn't afford it.

Image—buying the right stationery, wearing the right suit—all of that was important when we were starting out because those were the things they were judging us by. Everybody has these horror tales: I took some guy to a hundred-dollar lunch and he told me he'd been fired and was looking for a job. But it was important to spend my money as if it didn't matter because as soon as I said, "No, I'm not hungry, I'll just have an appetizer," I was finished. And I recognized that. It's part of the game.

Your Image Depends on Your Business

There's a whole other kind of business you can go into, and people like the idea of helping a nice young guy. I have a friend with a bunch of quick-copy centers in L.A. and he lives in a fabulous house in Malibu; he's making all this money but he doesn't tell anybody because part of *his* thing is people like the idea of helping this nice young kid selling Xerox copies. I think a lot depends on what your business is, the kind of people you're selling to.

Edward McCabe, ADVERTISING EXECUTIVE

Appearances Lend Credibility

I believe that, when lacking widespread credibility, appearances are very important because they add to a feeling that you have some credibility. But if you have credibility and you're very good and known for what you do, I don't think it matters where you work. In fact, the opposite can help you: the crazy scientist working in the garage.

Dr. Richard Winter, EXECUTIVE HEALTH EXAMINERS

Showing People What They Want to See

We always did marketing as a team, a businessman and a doctor. I always gave the impression that I really didn't want to discuss money; I was too interested in my microscope and laboratory animals and heart disease. The businessman would take care of that sort of thing. I came along to explain why sigmoidostomy was important, why a checkup was important, and why our quality was better. But when it came to quoting fees and prices, I'd say, "I'm a doctor." Of course I knew them very well; I had planned the whole thing to begin with. It goes over better with patients. Patients don't like to think of a doctor as a businessman. It is not good salesmanship to come across that way, particularly with businessmen.

Make the Client Feel Important

Businessmen enjoy chatting with a doctor. One of the reasons we have an executive dining room is we can invite big shots who come to the clinic here, president of this, chairman of that, to stay for lunch with the doctors. My theory was—and it happens to be true—that he could, with a snap of his fingers, summon up lawyers and other executives, his treasurer, his priest, to have lunch with him, but he couldn't get three or four doctors to sit around and have lunch with him; they weren't interested. The clients enjoy it tremendously.

BEYOND FIRST IMPRESSIONS

Jeffrey Feinman, PROMOTIONAL CONSULTANT

You Cannot Consistently Con Somebody over a Period of Time

Later, client relationships are more honest and everybody knows where everybody's coming from. All kinds of relationships—between nations, between men and women, between clients and suppliers—are a function of time. You cannot consistently con somebody over an extended period of time. In the beginning, in the honeymoon razzle-dazzle, there are a lot of different buttons you can try pushing on different people, but over a period of time our clients have a perfect sense about what's good and bad about us.

I personally have a reputation for losing things. A story was once repeated to me by a secretary: Somebody in the marketing department went up to the vice-president for marketing and said, "We really got to get rid of Ventura; this is the second time they've lost a piece of artwork." The VP said, "Look, Ventura's turned out the best stuff this company's ever seen—they've made millions of dollars for us. When you work with Jeff, you've got to assume that some of the time he's going to lose something." And I think that's the same kind of relationship you have with people; they're terrific, but you know that some of the time they're not going to show up. That's just the way they are. But in the beginning, a lot of those mirrors and addresses are really important.

Edward McCabe, ADVERTISING EXECUTIVE

Street Smarts

Being really tuned into people and the way they act and the way they think is a very big part of success. I think most formal education prevents people from being aware of that. I'm not trying to knock education; I wish I had had more, and I love to read and it's very important. But I think the whole structured aspect of education tends to make people less "street smart," if I may use the phrase, and I think you have to be street smart because it gives you a greater clue into what really makes people tick and the way they're going to react. If you learn everything by the books, that's not the real world, it doesn't always happen that way. What happens is, nine out of ten times, people will react in situations the way people react, and the books don't always tell you about that.

Jeffrey Hollender, NETWORK FOR LEARNING

Ideas Are the Hardest Things in the World to Sell

Whenever you're going to sell anything—or whenever I'm going to sit and write a Network for Learning course description—you have to put yourself in the place of the person who's going to read it. You don't write what sounds good or what you like or what makes sense to you, but you have to write with the reader in mind—what they're going to perceive, how that's going to make them feel, what that's going to make them think about. I've written some very beautiful things that I enjoy and love and that sound great and don't sell anything because they don't talk to anybody.

I would say that history has demonstrated that you can sell anything. You have to make it tangible. You can't sell an idea; you have to sell a benefit. You can't sell the concept of "How to Marry Money" [a Network course]. You've got to sell something tangible, which is: I'm going to tell you where to find someone with money who's looking to get married, I'm going to tell you what to say to them, what to do, how to act, how to dress. That's concrete.

"How to Flirt" is for me too abstract. So when I write

the course description, I talk about the benefits of flirting. I talk about being in a strange town and trying to get a check cashed and not having any ID. Or I talk about women in business. I talk about concrete applications. The same with "Social Climbing." What is "Social Climbing"? I try to apply social climbing to a struggling young artist trying to get into an art gallery, as well as someone who is trying to climb the corporate ladder, or someone who is a new member at a country club. You have to make it concrete, and you've got to select examples that people either find fanciful or that they can relate to as benefitting them personally.

Christopher Whittle, CHAIRMAN, *ESQUIRE* MAGAZINE

The Use of Compelling Imagery

I don't know if anybody else uses the concept of "compelling imagery"—it's my own label—and it simply is this. The world out there is full of all these messages being communicated in five thousand different ways, from telephone calls to letters to advertisements to personal visits to whatever. And in whatever you're doing, whether it's attempting to get somebody to buy a film script or to purchase a company or to sell a page of advertising, you have to determine: *What is the essence of* why *they should be interested?* and get it down to this one impactful position.

So often people walk in with a whole bag full of junk that they kind of throw on the desk and say, "Here are all the reasons you should do this," and when they leave the room, people don't remember anything, it was just kind of garbled. And the reason is, typically, that people don't prepare, they don't take the time to think things through from the other person's point of view, and to really come up with that concise statement. That's compelling imagery.

The World Likes Stories

The second thing is the means of communicating it. There are a couple of effective ways to communicate compelling imagery and I think the best is stories. The world likes stories, and if you have a concept that you are wanting to communicate and you can weave it into an interesting story, people listen. People like to listen that way. It's not a speech, it's not a lecture, it's the telling of something. If you can work what it is you're wanting to communicate into the story of its development or whatever it is, people get it. If you distill it down and dry it out, it doesn't come out nearly so well. That's a forgotten thing. I see whole industries that have forgotten that concept.

Jerry Rubin, BUSINESS NETWORKING SALONS

I think successful people see life as a movie. I think successful people are more influenced by stories and movies than unsuccessful people. I always look at my life as a movie. I don't have an ending in mind, but I have the fact that there are many possible endings. I'm able to see the cinematic possibilities.

John DePasquale, DIRECT MARKETING

Using a Catalogue to Tell a Story About the Products

We all have cycles, ups and downs. People are vulnerable at the peaks and valleys of their lives. If you are really irritated, you go out and you buy a new purse. When you're elated, you go out and buy something as a treat or a reward. So, our catalogue is a little manipulative; the reason behind using a story in the catalogue is not so much to play a little game of just having some editorial or showing something different, it's to start to create the character. It starts to pick up on the psychological head-set of a woman.

Conceptually, that's when you can break down brand loyalties, that's when you can present opportunities. That's when you can make a sale. The other thing that is strategically different about this catalogue is we have made the reader the heroine, not the product. In most catalogues, it's the product that is.

Listening to People

This catalogue is for the working woman. Catalogues are so right for the future. I'm thinking now of a catalogue for divorced and single men, about household products. How do you become efficient around the house? What is the difference between a six-cup coffeepot and a ten-cup coffeepot? This came up because I listened to people talk about our own catalogues, and I was looking at statements like, "A ten-cup coffeepot you can make six cups in, and each cup is perfect." I asked, "Do you have to say that?" All the women said, "Yes, yes, yes," and they all knew exactly what it meant. Not a man in the room knew what they were talking about.

Make the World Your Business

Try to understand what is going on and how that might relate to your business. If you start to see people walking around barefoot, that pretty much is going to have a disastrous effect on the shoe business. Well, what is that going to do to the rubber-sole business? And the fact that our client might be an owner of that kind of company? You have to start to some extent to be your own eyes and ears and to make the connections. That's the tricky part, obviously.

David Liederman, DAVID'S COOKIES

Catering to a Consumer's Impulse

Promoting is not what I'm all about. What I'm about is, I have a product to sell. People do not eat David, they eat David's Cookies.

My philosophy is, you get the people in, you serve them as courteously as possible, and you get them the hell out of the store and you wait on the next customer.

Cookies are an impulsive item. Most people walk by a cookie store and think, "I want those cookies, but I shouldn't eat them because I'm on a diet." Monday morning it's dead because everybody's on a diet Monday. The diet starts breaking down by Tuesday.

Macy's believes you stand there for two hours waiting in line because if you're waiting in line to buy the cookies, maybe you'll go buy something else. I guarantee they lose half their customers who think, "I can't eat these cookies, I'm trying to be on a diet."

FUNDAMENTAL BELIEFS

Edward McCabe, ADVERTISING EXECUTIVE

As far as pitching business is concerned, there are people involved, and even though you have fundamental beliefs, you have to tailor the nuances to the people. Some clients don't like to see people not wearing ties, so you wear a tie. You're not going against your beliefs; you do things different ways for different people.

But to me, the ultimate thing is in all of this—and this is going to sound very Mary Poppins—is to be totally honest at all times. Now, when I'm honest it's sometimes very undiplomatic. And other times, it's just honest. People relish that. They have to take it when it's

204 STARTING AT THE TOP

unpleasant in order to get it when it's pleasant, but they'll always know that it's honest.

There are people in all kinds of businesses who are deceitful, who stretch the truth, who are evasive, who are afraid to take a stand. I have a reputation for being very blunt. To me that's the secret to success. "Honesty is the best policy." It's cornball stuff. If you're always honest, sometimes they hate it. The last thing they want to hear is the truth, and "Go home," or "No." But if you don't do that, if you tell them what they want to hear, every time they hear what they want to hear they're going to doubt whether or not you mean it. And they're not, ultimately, going to trust you. If somebody can really always trust you, I think that's the best thing.

I've been involved in situations in my career where I thought it was important for the client to know something, and other people thought it was wiser not to let them know—and I always turned out to be right. I've only run into trouble with it once. I had a client, and he would avoid me and I would avoid him, because it was unpleasant. And one day some people here sold him a commercial that I told people I didn't think was a good commercial, that they shouldn't have sold it, and they said, no, he loved it, and now he really wanted to do it. We couldn't go and unsell him. That was my mistake. I should have at that point gone back and tried to unsell him, no matter how much I disliked spending a minute with him.

What I did was, a month later, after it was all done, I took him to lunch, and I said, "You really like that commercial?" and he said, "Yeah." And then he made the mistake of asking me if I liked it. And I said, "No." He became enraged. He said, "You let me spend my money on something you didn't like!" And I said, "Well, everybody told me you loved it and you never asked my opinion on anything before." For a month he ranted and raved about how I didn't tell him I didn't think something was good, and then he was fired. But I learned a lesson: I would have been better off being overhonest, no matter how unpleasant, than holding back and letting that go.

I think the main reason to be honest is, if you never lie, they'll always trust you, even if they don't want to hear the truth. But if you put candy on the truth to make it more palatable, it's not real.

Helen Boehm, BOEHM PORCELAIN

If people have something wonderful, they can crow about it, but it's got to be wonderful. They've got to be different, and if they don't have at least that, let them have beautiful service, let them deal honestly. Because you can't beat that. Then you can sleep at night. The day that you start worrying how you're going to connive, how you're going to shortchange this one or that one or the other one, steal this one's product or idea, you are just overtaxing yourself with deviousness, instead of creativity and quality.

The three *S*'s of marketing: You sell with your self and sincerity. Yourself is you, that's all you have. Every piece you sell with your name on it is you.

Edward McCabe, ADVERTISING EXECUTIVE

It comes back to that old, corny "To thine own self be true," and if somebody asked me to write down my philosophy, I probably couldn't because what it is is in myself. We won't take a cigarette account because I don't believe in it. Smoking them and selling them to people are two different things. Killing myself and doing it to other people are two different things. To me, that's very clear; I don't have to defend that one—it's obvious. Early in our business, our second account, they dictated what the advertising was going to be and we fired them. I said, No, I don't believe in it. And it was very hard then. We once handled a political candidate, and since then I've believed that that's bad, and now we won't handle a political candidate. You often don't get paid, but that's another reason for not taking them.

My feeling on a political candidate is this. If you sell a tube of toothpaste that's no good, somebody's going to get a cavity. You sell them a President that's no good and you're going to get killed. The stakes are altogether different. I won't sell a tube of toothpaste if I know it isn't any good, but sometimes you make a mistake. And with a political candidate, the problem is you become a zealot, and you believe that that's right but you don't know any more than you know about the toothpaste. The best soap, the best chicken: I can convince myself that that's true and if it turns out that my beliefs were not real, what's the ultimate harm done? But you do that with the wrong President or a senator—no, I wouldn't want that responsibility. It's making a mistake for other people; I'm not worried about myself.

John DePasquale, DIRECT MARKETING

Personal Ethics Are Business Ethics

You never know when people and things are going to crop up next, and you walk the straight and narrow, so to speak. That is my personal philosophy.

Richard Leibner, AGENT

Good Advice

Be honest; don't get caught in lies. Sometimes you fudge in the gray. I do so many things that keeping track of one set of facts is difficult; to keep track ot two sets of facts is impossible. If you tell the truth, you can't ever get in trouble. There are ways to hedge and fudge, to conceal, to strategize, and to do things. The only time you get in trouble is when you out-and-out lie. It's not like you're making one deal your whole life and you lie and cheat because this is the whole roll of the dice. If you are a newscaster, and I lie for you this afternoon, and I lose credibility making a fifty-thousand-dollar deal for you, I'm damaging 150 other people who shouldn't retain me to do their next deal if I can't have the same reputation I had when I did it for them before. I think we have the lowest dropout rate, the lowest loss rate in the agency business. And that's really what's important.

Jeffrey Feinman, PROMOTIONAL CONSULTANT

Foolproof Technique

Although it sounds hokey and trite, the easiest selling technique in this society—it's absolutely foolproof—is to give people what you promise them. We're in a service business. If you think about it, there's nothing we do that the client can't do for himself. I don't mean that you could take out your own appendix. But the idea that Doubleday comes to Jeff Feinman to get a book printed is somewhat bizarre. They know where the printers are, they know where to buy paper. But in a world where nobody means Tuesday morning when they say Tuesday morning, delivering what you promised when you promised it is a lifelong assurance.

If you screw someone once, there's no money in it. The money's in doing forty promotions. The secret of our business is to give the client more than they paid for and they will come back time and time again. We don't have trouble—save our share of screwups—keeping clients because we honor deadlines. That's how I select people. It sounds hokey and trite, but we've built this business on one thing: We can be counted on. What we say we'll do, we do.

The ability to get the job done is a commodity in short supply in America.

VITAL DETAILS

Dr. Richard Winter, EXECUTIVE HEALTH EXAMINERS

Packaging

Packaging is important, the total look of the product is important. We are known as the quality place in the world to have these examinations done; it sells this company. If you go to our clinic, you'll notice patients all in white, and they have badges with their names. The personnel are trained to treat them carefully, they are called by name, this kind of thing.

There are a lot of details that have been perfected over the years. We treat everybody here like an executive even if they're a Pullman car conductor. There's a butler in the locker room who helps them with their clothes. It's those things—attention to detail, which I pride myself in— I think make it successful. The way a patient is handled is what the answer is.

George Lang, RESTAURATEUR

Packaging/Presentation

Gimbel's or Macy's—I'm not sure which one it was— a couple of decades ago made history by taking mink coats and throwing them on a big table in the middle of the aisle, in the basement—what they used to do with seconds, sweaters that they couldn't sell for three years. And to everybody's amazement, they sold more the first day than they'd sold in months or years.

Context

The girl in the convertible always looks much prettier than she is. When she suddenly leaves the convertible, you're surprised how plain she is. I could go on with the various parallels, allegories, scattershot-style, but what I'm trying to say, really, is that putting an individual, a place, an organization, an idea, an object, into certain situations under a certain type of lighting, with certain surroundings—certain setting is really what I'm saying—and presenting it as another thing, is a very pleasant experience and it's kind of a perceptional displacement, if I may coin a stupid word. Perceptional displacement, because on the table suddenly the mink coat becomes a big bargain that you can afford even if you can't afford it, not an extraordinary luxury that you should wait for for twenty years. And the girl in the convertible, with the aura lent by the Cadillac, suddenly becomes something in our mind, in our perception, which she really is not.

I presented this little jewel of a place as a neighborhood restaurant. There is some justification to it; if I had done it with The Four Seasons, I would have fallen flat, because Park Avenue and Fifty-Second Street is not a neighborhood. They'd have laughed me out of town. In this case, it had some very sound justification. This is bedroomsville, New York City. By calling this little jewel a neighborhood restaurant, I allow people to come to a pretty place daily without feeling that they're going to some real fancy place. It became their hangout, it became their place.

Christopher Whittle, CHAIRMAN, *ESQUIRE* MAGAZINE

Small Touches

Small touches make big differences. I think a lot of people think that if you're a big businessman you don't pay attention to details. I really think very much differently: Whether you *personally* pay attention to them or not, you are constantly concerned with the small touches on things because it's what differentiates, usually, quality from less quality. Details down to, if you're making a presentation to a group, how the chairs are organized, because this affects how people feel. Six straight rows of chairs are so different from kind of an arced grouping. That's a small example, but the experience that people have in that situation versus the other is different.

In the beginning you can personally deal with three hundred things that are important. Those three hundred grow into thirty thousand and there's no way that you can deal with these, so you have to build into your organization a sense of detail, and of the importance of detail, and that it is attention to detail that differentiates. I think people who do things really well know that.

Otto Bettman, BETTMANN ARCHIVE

Only the Best

I have all through my life had an obsession—which is rather paradoxical for a picture lover—I love to throw pictures away. I do believe that in order to serve the people who use pictures, you must keep the chaff from the wheat.

I have always prided myself on only keeping pictures that really responded to all the requirements of a good picture—good design, good reproducibility, emotional appeal, and so on. I was reminded of this saying by some rock dealer who said he knew rocks. He said, "Rocks are afraid of me. They tremble when they see me." I have always tried to only keep the best. From this kind of editorial distillation, which we have practiced, the Bettmann Archive has taken on a certain status, the Tiffany of the picture business. This inclination to aim for the cream of the crop has enabled me to be quite friendly with a lot of other archives. While there are other picture collections than the Bettmann Archive, my collection is simply much easier, more accessible.

David Liederman, DAVID'S COOKIES

Keep It Simple

I learned about good food when I was working at Troisgros in France, where we were doing some of the best food in the world. And the main thing I learned about it, working in a great French kitchen, is that everything we did was incredibly simple. We were just doing very simple things very well. If we were roasting a chicken, we would roast the chicken very well. If we were broiling a lobster, we would do that very well, and if we were frying French fries, we would do that better than anybody else.

So I realized that the best ideas were often the simplest, and that everybody's trying to build a better mousetrap by reinventing the mousetrap; maybe you should make the original mousetrap work a little better. So my basic philosophy was to just offer a simple product.

SELLING STYLES

Christopher Whittle, CHAIRMAN, *ESQUIRE* MAGAZINE

Sales as Problem Solving

We have tried to elevate the whole concept of selling. I think that *salesman* has come to mean something in the world, and a lot of things it's come to mean are not particularly positive. And for some good reason, because I think sales, because of how some people go about it, is not a pleasant experience, either for the salesman or for the person who's getting sold.

A Creative Experience

There's a whole other way to approach sales, which is really attempting to problem-solve with the other person involved, to solve both your problems and truly to make a deal where both parties benefit. It's a much more creative approach, it's much more fun for both parties, because the person who is the seller does not feel he is imposing and the person who is being sold does not feel he is being imposed upon. And so often that is the relationship. It's not even a relationship, it's the "encounter." We have spent a lot of time trying to turn that experience into a creative experience.

We don't can speeches, and we don't send people out on missions to situations that really they shouldn't be sent out on—which a lot of companies do. For example, there are a lot of companies that attempt to say their product is for everybody. Usually products aren't, and it's much better to only try to convince people that your products make sense when they do make sense and not when they don't. And if there's no one to go to, then we've got a bad product, and forget the product.

Wally "Famous" Amos

What You're Always Selling Is Yourself

I think the Famous Amos idea and I were perfect for one another. I think, though, that I can sell anything I believe in, anything that is substance, because what you're always selling is yourself. You're never selling the product; you're selling yourself.

Anyone who can promote can be a success. You can be a success for a minute, but if you want to sustain, there has to be some integrity. There has to be some value and some quality to what it is that you're selling, that you're promoting; otherwise I don't think that you're going to last.

David Liederman, DAVID'S COOKIES

If They Won't Buy It, Give Them Something Else

At Forty-second Street we're going to sell pizza. I could probably sell *anything* on Forty-second Street; it's one of the most heavily populated areas in the world. I'll find something to sell there. The theory is, if you put a show on Broadway and the show doesn't work, what do you do, knock down the theatre? No, you change the show. Well, it's the same thing with the restaurant business. The restaurant doesn't work, you change the restaurant, you give people something else. I subscribe to that theory, except I believe you should offer the public a better product than anybody else, because then you have a good location *and* you have a better product.

Lois Wyse, ADVERTISING EXECUTIVE

Buying Is Emotional

I really think you have to totally believe in what you're selling. And if you totally believe in what you're selling, and if you get your facts together, and if you present a rational argument, you can sell anything. Most buying is emotional, and all people need is a rational reason for following their emotions.

So give people the facts first and then give them the freedom to respond emotionally.

A Good Line

There isn't a campaign we present for which we don't first lay the groundwork, the *reasons* for what we're doing. I think that's really the key. The best story is how the line "With a name like Smucker's, it has to be good" was written. Marc [Wyse] said to me one day, "You know, we've been handling Smucker's for a couple of years and we still haven't come up with a good line." I said, "Well, I can come up with a good line, but then you have to sell it," because he was the account man and I was the creative person. He said, "Give it to me and I can sell it." I said, "I have a line, I know exactly what to do." I went to the typewriter and sat down and wrote, "With a name like Smucker's, it has to be good," and then wrote a piece of copy that went with it, because, as I said, everything always has to have a reason. The copy said, "We could have named our jelly anything we wanted. We could have called it, 'Grandmother's Preserves,' or 'Ye Olde Jam Pot.' We were so proud of what we put inside the jelly that we put our name on the jar." That was the whole philosophy of it.

Marc took that piece of copy and we did it as a newspaper ad. We took it down to Smucker's and showed it to them. The sales manager looked at it and said to Paul Smucker, "If you ever go with that line, we'll be out of business in six months." But Marc was persistent—he's a very good salesman—and they finally agreed they would try the line in California because they didn't have any relatives there.

So they ran the campaign in California on radio, with Mason Adams. Paul Smucker got on a plane from Cleveland to Los Angeles, and the stewardess asked for his name. He said, "Smucker," and she said, "Oh, with a name like Smucker's, it has to be good." So he didn't need the plane to get out there. He went to the hotel and they asked his name and the same thing happened. He got into all the hard-to-get-into restaurants. He called Marc from California and said, "We'll let the relatives collect the dividends, and let's use that campaign everywhere." Today that's the longest-running campaign in American advertising.

Richard Leibner, AGENT

Keep 'Em Guessing

Sometimes you soft-sell, sometimes you hard-sell. I used to say, "We're just the soft-sell," but you do such a volume with the same number of people over and over, sometimes you're soft, sometimes you're hard. The best thing to be is a little unpredictable, so when you walk in the room, the guy doesn't know if you're going to be in a little bit of a screaming mood or a joke-telling mood.

Why I think we've done as well as we have is not only are we trusted by our clients, but we're trusted by management, because we deal with situations realistically and do not lie.

It's Passion

Some people will tell you I'm the biggest pain in the ass, scrounging for another $25 a week—this is the same agent who makes a million-dollar deal. You're goddamn right. I'll fight longer and harder for that last $1300 for somebody making $30,000, $40,000. It's easier for the big hitters because management pays the big hitters. It's having as much passion for doing a $35,000 job as for doing a $150,000 job.

Nate Bienstock (my former partner) used to play a game that was a good training tool. When he would go into a negotiation with someone he had worked with for years, he'd write down on a piece of paper where he thought the deal should close, and the other guy would write down where he thought the deal should close, and very often they were very close to each other. They wouldn't open up the pieces of paper till the end of an hour of fighting, after starting from totally different positions. But they had gotten to know each other.

Jeffrey Feinman, PROMOTIONAL CONSULTANT

Doing It All

The biggest single cost we have is the sales call. What I need to do is find out everything that the product manager at Life Savers can buy and then sell them everything so that they can throw away their Rolodex, so they can buy their celebrities from us, their ballpoint pens, whatever. We have the connections. They trust us, we get the job done. "What else can we sell you?" It pierces our hearts when someone says, "I just bought a shirt at Macy's." "You bought a shirt and you didn't call us to quote on it?"

David Brown, FILM PRODUCER

I tend to unburden myself.

I just do what I feel. I'm not an actor. I don't have a game plan, and so I'm afraid I go in not wholly prepared, but I go by my instincts, by my emanations, by the vibes. I don't go in with a scenario. If I make a speech, I have notes, but I generally depart from them.

My plan for negotiation is never to make the best deal for anything. In other words, if you are selling me a story, I don't offer you less money than I've been authorized to offer. I try to say, "Let's do it for that amount, this is what I've got." I think that creative people, unlike that great aphorism of Oscar Wilde's, *do* know the value as well as the price of everything. Business types don't as a rule. I hate haggling.

In the case of *The Sting,* Richard Zanuck and I overbid our own studio, Universal, because we could see we were going to lose that project to MGM. Universal was our partner, handling the business affairs. We told Universal we'd put up one hundred thousand dollars of our own money, to be deducted from the fees that were payable to us over the next three years. We weren't satisfied with the bid Universal had made and we thought we would lose the project, but that's all they would agree to do. We gave them one hundred thousand dollars.

Jeffrey Feinman, PROMOTIONAL CONSULTANT

Get On with It

It's take the money now. I used to be the original holdout for the last dollar. A friend taught me to say, "Fine," and close. Just do it and get on to the next project rather than keep a thousand things hanging. It's closing the deal. Most people love to have lunches, conversations, meetings—and never get anything accomplished. We have at any given time probably nine hundred projects going here. It's do it, get on to the next thing.

Richard Leibner, AGENT

I love one-liners. People call all day long to tell them to me. I use them in negotiations, tell jokes to change the pace in conversation. People never know where I'm coming from or what I'm going to say next.

A SYSTEMATIC APPROACH

Jeffrey Hollender, NETWORK FOR LEARNING

Preparation

The greatest key to success, whenever you do anything, whenever you go into a meeting, is knowing where you want to go, where you want to be at the end of the meeting. You know what you want the person you're meeting with to say, to agree to. You have to sit down and think through: "Well, if they say this, what am I going to say? If they say that, what am I going to say?" And you can plan the whole thing out in advance. I find, more than anything else, that gets me to where I want to go. Whether you want to hire someone, fire someone, sign a contract, get out of a contract, whatever it is.

Most people don't really have the discipline to, in your mind—and you don't even have to do it on paper, but in your mind—carry out the whole scenario. "What am I going to do if the person doesn't show up? If they're late? If they say this or that?" You can bring your creativity and everything you have to it when you're sitting in your office by yourself, but when you're there across the table from someone, and all of a sudden they say something you're not expecting to hear, and you have to then on the spot make a decision, the chances of making the wrong decision are much, much higher. I try to think through everything I do in advance. That's a great help.

Christopher Whittle, CHAIRMAN, *ESQUIRE* MAGAZINE

Timing

One of the things that's been particularly helpful to me is an understanding of time.

I think that all things have gestation periods and those cycles just can't be shortened. There basically aren't shortcuts, and if you develop a sense of the timing, you have a very valuable trait because it so helps you in planning. I think in five- and seven-year frames, because I know that's how long some things take. And on other things I think in three-month frames.

In a general sense, let's say that you want to get someone or an organization to do something. You have to develop a sense of the proper flow that's required and that they need to experience whatever it is for a period of time, become accustomed to it, feel comfortable with it, contribute to it. So much in the world is a rush job, and it's because whoever's trying to rush the job has not figured out that there is a sequence. What they do is they misplace urgency; they put it in the wrong place. Urgency should always be the first thing, and it is almost always the last, and back-end urgency is kind of desperate energy that's blown; it's never effective.

I believe people work well under deadlines, but what I do is pull the deadlines way up. In other words, if this is the event, there are certain deadlines that are back here—a year or two years back here—not out there. And just leaving the time to accomplish things correctly—placing the urgency early, where you say, "I've got to deal with this," or "That won't happen in eighteen months if . . ." That is something that has served me well. I try to teach it in our own company, and I think larger institutions have institutionalized it, meaning that somewhere the institution has picked up on it, and the whole concept of strategic-planning departments are people who understand that you must look ahead. So clearly, I do think it's a trait that successful people share.

Lists and Priorities

I think lists and prioritization are crucial to success: Again, this has been in my field. I have whole systems. There's always a day list, and a week list, and a six-month-period list—it's a constant rotating thing and there's no way I could function without them. I think there are people who function without them, but I don't think you function as well, because I don't think you can get to those small touches, because there are so many of them that if you're not watching them, you can't hold them in your head.

First of all, when you set priorities, you realize you're not going to get it all done. So the first form of prioritization is: What are you going to do? There are going to be certain things you never get done, and usually those are the *really* small touches.

Otto Bettmann, BETTMANN ARCHIVE

Order

I have been very fortunate that I have an overwhelming interest in music, and it has brought me to this new project, a biography of Bach. There was a great principle of order in everything in Bach, and I took piano lessons from the time I was six, and was trained to do things right, to break things up, complicated problems, measure by measure. One man who visited the Bettmann Archive one time said, "You must admit there's a lot of Bach in the Bettman Archive." The orderly system: Nothing succeeds until there is a logic to it. The structure stands by itself.

John DePasquale, DIRECT MARKETING

I am a very methodical person. I am very systems, procedures oriented, and I built this company that way. I ask that the people here be somewhat attendant to structure, discipline, without being the proverbial white shirt, gray-flannel suit. So I like to foster an entrepreneurial spirit within a certain amount of regimentation. I don't believe in chaos as the answer.

Wally "Famous" Amos

Maintaining Consistency and Quality

You just have to stay on top of it. But that's with anything: You can take nothing for granted. Everything needs to be nurtured and given attention. I don't care what it is you're doing. You just leave it alone and it's going to be taken away. You're making shoes, you're making shirts, it doesn't matter. Whatever it is. You got to stay on top. You got to support the people that are doing it, you got to encourage the people that are doing it. You got to let them know, you got to give them direction.

EMOTIONS

Jeffrey Hollender, NETWORK FOR LEARNING

Bad-Times Advice

When things are going poorly and you're feeling down and you're feeling like things aren't going to work out— that is the worst time to try to make any kind of major decision. When things are going poorly, the best thing you can do is, whatever the problem is, try to resolve it. Don't start reconsidering everything you're doing or your whole project or your whole life, because things always look different a day or two later, once you've overcome that difficulty. People make that mistake all the time: One thing goes wrong and they then call everything into question. Both personally and in business that happens to a lot of people.

David Liederman, DAVID'S COOKIES

It's Not the Name

If you're in business, you cannot have your ego in your business. You strive to do two things: stay alive and make a living, and deliver a good product, which is directly tied into whether you're going to stay alive and make a living. If I got crazy about taking down a David's sign because it's my name, then you could check me into Bellevue tomorrow. Because that's just not what it's all about. I tend to keep a low profile. We just run the business. The only thing I care about is whether the cookies keep on selling.

Jerry Rubin, BUSINESS NETWORKING SALONS

Keeping Ego in Its Place

You make a lot of mistakes, but you can't pay attention to your mistakes. I made a mistake today, I made a mistake yesterday. I think it's important not to get emotional in business. I think it's also very important to ignore the negative and just keep your mind on the purpose of the game, which is making money. For example, let's say you get into an emotional thing with somebody. Well, then you have to ask yourself, "Is this important? This is ego. The important thing is improving sales."

There's good ego and bad ego. First of all, you shouldn't care about how much money anyone else is making so long as you're doing OK. A lot of people hurt themselves because they want to hurt someone else. You've got to be positive, because if you're positive, then you can feel good about other people. A lot of people can get angry about something, come out with the negative. That's the whole thing about lawyers—people get involved with lawsuits to put themselves right and they spend a hundred thousand dollars. It's a bad business decision.

Mobilize the good ego. The good ego is the ego that has an ideal, an idea, that wants to serve people's needs. The bad ego is the ego that compares, that says, "He screwed me." Yeah, people are going to screw you; so let people screw you. Or, "I lost money." You're going to lose money.

XI. BIOGRAPHIES

WALLY "FAMOUS" AMOS

"I've used every experience I've ever had to sell chocolate-chip cookies," says Wally Amos, founder of Famous Amos. Early training at New York City's Food Trades Vocational High School was a good beginning, but even more beneficial were the years Amos spent as a theatrical agent and manager. The success of the cookies, now sold nationwide in department stores, supermarkets, and Famous Amos shops is, above all, a lesson in promotion. From organizing "debuts" to hosting birthday parties for the cookie, Amos never stops promoting his product.

The Svengali of the gourmet-cookie industry explains, "I gave the cookie a personality. I made this cookie really happy, energetic, friendly. It was a show-business concept; I *managed* the cookie. It's a star. I'd been in show business fourteen years, so all I did was transfer this concept to the cookie."

After serving in the Air Force and holding various civilian jobs, Amos was hired as the first black agent-trainee at the William Morris Agency, and later became a personal manager for musicians and film clients.

For years, friends had given Amos's cookies the highest accolades: "You should *sell* these." So when Amos decided he'd had enough of show business and "just wanted to make a living," he opened a shop in Los Angeles in 1975. He received backing from Helen Reddy, Jeff Wald, Artie Mogull, and the late Marvin Gaye. The business was a success from the first day, and Amos is often credited with kicking off what has become a five billion-dollar gourmet-cookie industry.

OTTO BETTMANN

Curator emeritus of the Bettmann Archive, Otto Bettmann fled to this country from Nazi Germany in 1935. The two steamer trunks crammed with prints and miniature photographs he carried with him would provide the basis for the Bettmann Archive, a visual library that supplies publishers, designers, artists, and advertisers with rare and unusual pictures. The Archive now contains over five thousand major categories, from nuclear disasters to artificial teeth to strange births, and is nothing short of a history of civilization.

Bettmann began his collecting as an avocation. As a child, he would reclaim from wastepaper baskets the curious pictures his physician father received as advertisements from pharmaceutical houses. His instinct to transport his trove to America was prompted by a desire to continue the scholarly and curatorial work he had pursued in Germany. However, his arrival here coincided with the advent of pictorial journalism, the heyday of *Life* and *Time* magazines, and despite his academic's aversion to business, Bettmann began to supply his prints to this eager market. For almost fifty years he has continued to collect and discard pictures. Furthermore, the system is sound from a business perspective; once a picture is in the Archive, it can be used again and again.

The immigrant Bettmann sees his success as indigenous to America. "Even in Germany, I always liked America. I had this incredible feeling of its greatness, of its marvelous fertile soil, that a man with such a crazy idea as to establish an archive could really succeed. Now, you could not do that in France very well. Here you can simply print a letterhead and you are in business. That's something that is so incredible in America, readiness to accept ideas, and the searching for them."

Bettmann is now retired and living in Florida, where he teaches history courses at a local university and is working on a biography of Bach. He has written or collaborated on nine books, including *The Good Old Days: They Were Terrible!*, which is a pictorial reminder of how rough things were in those good old days.

HELEN BOEHM

At the end of World War II, Helen Boehm and her husband, Edward Marshall Boehm, set up a studio in Trenton, New Jersey, to produce porcelain figures. He had been sculpting porcelain animals as a hobby, and with the encouragement and aid of his wife, now began to pursue his craft full-time. Funded by an investment of one thousand dollars, the couple began their business. Edward Boehm designed, and Helen, who gave up her job as an optician (she was the first woman optician licensed to practice in New York), took over the administration and marketing. Since her husband's death several years ago, Helen Boehm has run the company herself.

Boehm porcelain, displayed in New York's Metropolitan Museum of Art, the White House, and museums and palaces throughout the world, is now indisputably the foremost name in American porcelain. But for years the couple had to struggle simply to get their product recognized.

"First I'd started showing my husband's porcelain to the stores, the various lovely galleries in New York. But they'd never heard of Boehm, and said it would take a hundred years. So I knew I had to take a shortcut—because the quality was there, the good sculpture. But how do you convince Tiffany? So I thought, Let me first try getting it into the Museum." Boehm succeeded in her plan, and in 1951 the Metropolitan Museum put two of her husband's pieces in its collection.

While traveling around the country trying to place her husband's figures in stores, Boehm continued her efforts toward public recognition of the work. Her plan succeeded: Gifts of the porcelain to Presidents (beginning with Eisenhower), and to royalty (she gave a replica bridal bouquet to the Princess of Wales) have kept Boehm in the headlines and in the finest stores in the world.

Mrs. Boehm insists that for all the publicity and fanfare, it was a "four-letter word" that brought her success: *work*.

MARY BOONE

After graduating from the Rhode Island School of Design, Mary Boone came to New York City with the intention of becoming an artist. To support herself she took a job in a gallery. "I literally fell into the job. I had never really heard of or thought about the function of an art dealer. Even though I had known about art from early in life, I had never thought, How do these paintings get here?"

From this chance start, Boone fashioned a career that she now sees as the one she was ideally suited for from the start. "I became an art dealer just by virtue of having a job at a gallery. And I'd say three years into that I realized I could be, at best, only a good artist, and I thought even at that time I might have the capabilities of being much more realized as an art dealer."

She is now recognized as one of the most important dealers in contemporary art. When the uptown gallery she was working for closed, Boone, then twenty-five, opened her own gallery in a prime downtown location. Although offered opportunities to deal for other galleries, Boone chose to work for herself and to take on those contemporary artists whose work she wanted to promote. Her gallery represents the work of artists David Salle, Eric Fischl, Georg Baselitz, Jean-Michel Basquiat, and others in the forefront of contemporary art.

DAVID BROWN

Not content to excel in one field, David Brown has more than once undertaken a new career upon reaching the top position in his current one. Brown, sixty-nine, acknowledges this penchant for reordering his life every so often. "I've had a lot of careers. I've never grown old in one, although I'm in the process of growing old in movies. I've been a lobbyist, newspaperman, managing editor. I wrote horoscopes, I wrote jokes for Eddie Cantor. I was a gag writer for radio, edited books, had every job conceivable in the motion-picture industry. And then back to book publishing. I have been willing to change the course of my life every ten or fifteen years. Was it by plan? No. I don't know what lesson there is here, except that you don't have to do one thing all your life."

He has served as editor-in-chief of *Liberty Magazine,* founded *Femme,* the precursor of *Cosmopolitan* (a success story in its own right, now run by his wife, Helen Gurley Brown). His film credits include such classics as *The Sound of Music* (1965), *Patton* (1970), *The French Connection* (1971)—all of which received Oscars as Best Picture—*Butch Cassidy and the Sundance Kid* (1969), and *M*A*S*H* (1970).

Since forming an independent production company with Richard Zanuck in 1972, Brown has been responsible for *The Sting* (1973), *Jaws* (1975), *Jaws II* (1978), and most recently, *The Verdict* (1982). Along the way, Brown has published several books and articles, and continues to write and teach.

The only common thread through Brown's successes he sums up as, "I've always felt that if I had an office and a pad of paper, I would think of something. And that's always been true."

NOLAN BUSHNELL

Video-game pioneer Nolan Bushnell has founded four companies, sold two, and participated in the inception of several others since leaving the University of Utah seventeen years ago with a degree in engineering. Pong, Bushnell's first electronic game, was the cornerstone of Atari, Inc., the company he sold to Warner Communications for twenty-eight million dollars in 1976. After a couple of years with Warner's, Bushnell became impatient with the corporate mentality—"innovate me some like you did last year"—and left to work on his newest idea, Pizza Time Theatre.

Pizza Time was Bushnell's gambit for entering the operations end of the video-game business. His plan was to establish a chain of restaurant/game-arcades that would draw entire families rather than just teenagers. While patrons are waiting to be served, (nonunionized) robots entertain small children as older siblings pour quarters into video games. In 1982, the restaurants were opening at a rate of one every five days.

Pizza Time allowed Bushnell to enter the arcade business on his own terms. "Traditionally, game centers had to be in high-traffic locations, which are very, very expensive pieces of real estate. I said, 'I don't want to play that game. I want the world to come to me.' " So he made his own traffic, and brought the world—and their quarters—to him. He eventually left that business as well, again to move on to other ventures.

To Bushnell, all of these enterprises are extensions of a single idea, based on his understanding of systems. "Building systems is just changing your Tinkertoy set." Another Bushnell project is Catalyst Technologies, a system, as he puts it, designed to make companies. Catalyst was founded in 1981 to aid high-technology companies during their formation periods, using what Bushnell and his colleagues learned the hard way during their own start-up days. In exchange for Catalyst's assistance— funds, facilities, counsel—the company retains equity in the start-ups.

Under the auspices of Catalyst, Bushnell has recently created a home-entertainment company, Axlon Games.

HAL DAVID

Hal David credits the U.S. Army with turning him into a songwriter. Prior to a stint in the armed services, he had studied to become a journalist. While on duty in Hawaii, however, David became involved in producing musical shows, and when he returned to civilian life it was not to his old job at the *New York Post* but to pursue a career as a lyricist.

Dionne Warwick's is the voice and Burt Bacharach's the music most often associated with David's hits. "One Less Bell to Answer," "I Say a Little Prayer," "Walk On By," "Do You Know the Way to San Jose?" and "What the World Needs Now Is Love" were all million-seller records. For his work in films, David received an Academy Award ("Raindrops Keep Fallin' on My Head"), as well as several nominations ("Alfie," "What's New, Pussycat," "The Look of Love"), and for his work in theater was awarded a Grammy for the Broadway show *Promises, Promises*.

A different form of accolade was conferred upon him in 1980, when he was elected president of the

American Society of Composers, Authors and Publishers (ASCAP). As head of the oldest performing-rights licensing body in the country, David oversees the rights and benefits of the group's members. While working full-time in this position, David continues to write songs.

JOHN DePASQUALE

After graduating from the Wharton business school, John DePasquale joined one of the Big Eight accounting firms, knowing that ultimately he wanted to go into business for himself. Today, he not only works for himself, but has over three hundred employees working for him as well. In the decade since it was founded, De-Pasquale's DM Group has become the largest independent direct-marketing company in the country.

While still employed full-time at Arthur Young, De-Pasquale became involved with a new magazine being published for MBA students. To demonstrate to advertisers the magazine's effectiveness with readers, De-Pasquale undertook a direct-mail project. Response to the campaign was so great that he increased these activities, and eventually saw that this was the direction he wanted to take. "In the mid-sixties direct mail wasn't even an industry at all, so we were going to get in on the ground floor."

In 1974 he took his ideas and went into business for himself. The company has grown steadily since then, and now not only designs direct-mail and direct-marketing programs for clients, but also implements the campaigns as well, handling virtually all aspects of the projects from creative work to printing to mailing.

DePasquale's latest project is a shoppers' catalogue, *Access,* which provided the basis for a cable television show that featured the catalogue products and allowed for instantaneous telephone purchases.

JOHN DIEBOLD

John Diebold invented the concept of *automation,* and can also claim credit for having invented the word—or malapropism—as we know it. As a project on manufacturing at the Harvard business school, Diebold designed a plan for "automating" a factory. As automation did not at that time exist, neither did the word. The correct word would have been *automatization,* but faulty typing and poor spelling led Diebold to shorten the word to *automate.* "One of the people we'd been getting advice from at Harvard despised the word because he said it derived in part from Latin, and in part from Greek. He said, 'There's no future in this; it's like automobile, the same origins.' "

Both word and concept gained currency when Diebold published a book based on his study at Harvard, *Automation,* in 1952; thirty years later the book remains a classic in the field and has been reissued by the American Management Association. In 1954 he founded the Diebold Group, Inc., one of the first, and now one of the most highly respected, management-consulting firms in the world, and which specializes in the implementation of new technologies and systems. Diebold has made a career out of designing innovations for businesses, governments, and academic institutions.

JEFFREY FEINMAN

Jeffrey Feinman's success in the sales-promotion/ sweepstakes business was presaged in his childhood; the forty-one-year-old head of Ventura Associates, a leader in the promotion field, recalls that he "was always entering contests as a kid, was always caught up in that stuff. I never stopped saving Popsicle wrappers."

The wrappers now arrive in volume at his "fulfillment

center," the place where box tops and quarters are redeemed for T-shirts. In addition to running promotions, Ventura operates sweepstakes and contests for airlines, cigarette companies, banks, and other clients, many of which are on the *Fortune* 500 list. Feinman offers a broad definition of what constitutes a promotion, and his business, as "something extra the consumer did not expect to receive in the course of doing business." Specifically, it is Feinman's business to come up with ways to make money for his clients.

Having reached the position of vice-president in a marketing firm at the age of twenty-eight, Feinman discovered that, since the president of the company seemed to be in good health, "there was nowhere left to go." So he left to start up a company that would compete with his former employer's. He reasoned that if he was going to be working eighteen-hour days, he should be working eighteen-hour days for himself.

MILTON GLASER

His work on exhibit from New York's Museum of Modern Art to Grand Union supermarkets nationwide, Milton Glaser is one of the most accomplished and popular graphic designers in America. His projects have included cofounding with Clay Felker and designing *New York* magazine, redesigning *Esquire* magazine, consulting on the renovation of the Barbizon-Plaza Hotel in New York, and designing the observation deck at the World Trade Center. Glaser also teaches, and operates a commercial studio employing thirty designers. For a time he wrote a restaurant column, "The Underground Gourmet," and throughout it all has continued to pursue his art and illustration work.

Glaser suggests that his prolific and varied career is based on the need people have to "keep themselves alive to their work by not repeating their own history. I basically change what I do, the nature of what I do. I started out more or less as a kind of comic illustrator when I was very young, and then I moved to illustration in general. Then I became interested in design and went into the book jacket–design business, and I started doing things like posters. We started to do a large range of corporate work and trademarks and stuff, and then went into the magazine business at the same time. In recent years I've been doing more interior design—supermarkets and food-related projects, packaging. I just sort of keep moving along.''

JEFFREY HOLLENDER

Information is the latest in a succession of products for which consumers will gladly part with their disposable and not so disposable incomes. Such was the canny observation of Jeffrey Hollender, founder and president of Network for Learning, a program that offers adult courses such as "How to Flirt," "The Art of Social Climbing," "Careers in Cable TV," "How to Lose Your Brooklyn Accent," "How to Marry Money," and approximately 194 other single-session or month-long classes on topics not covered by conventional educational institutions.

Hollender makes no claims about education; his methods are hit and run and designed as much for fun as for self-improvement. Classes are "informationally rather than educationally oriented." They are, in addition, consumer oriented: students are treated as customers, and it is their satisfaction rather than their edification that is sought. The teachers are professionals in the areas that they teach—investment banking, advertising, cooking.

Hollender should perhaps consider teaching a course,

"How to Operate an Adult-Education Program." Network, started in 1979 with sixty classes attended by four hundred students, now attracts and instructs roughly sixty thousand people a year in its New York "classrooms"—lofts, restaurants, television studios. In addition, Hollender's company runs classes in Houston and anticipates franchises in several other cities around the country.

From his initial investment of sixty-thousand dollars, Hollender is now reaping the profits generated by video tapes, books, and audio cassettes, the material for which is provided by the classes; Hollender has maximized his profits by marketing one solid idea in very many ways. His overhead is minimized by handling everything on a "free agent" basis; the company has no teachers on staff, no real estate to support, refuting the theory that it is cheaper to buy than to rent.

NORMA KAMALI

O.M.O., the name of Norma Kamali's New York boutique and also of her line of couture wear, stands for *On My Own*. Kamali, forty, is on her own by virtue of both her independence and her originality. Her unmistakable designs cut from sweatshirt fabric in over-size proportions have received rare distinction: The are favored alike by the fashion industry (a Coty award in 1981), celebrities (Raquel Welch and Farrah Fawcett), and department-store shoppers.

Kamali's early ambition was to be a painter; as a compromise with her mother, she studied fashion illustration at New York's Fashion Institute of Technology. Unable to find work as an illustrator, she took a job as an airline clerk, and in the course of regular trips to London, became interested in design. She opened her first boutique, Kamali, Ltd., with her former husband (whose name she retains), in the sixties.

Her company's growth resulted from popular demand; *Cosmopolitan* magazine featured one of her radically cut swimsuits on its cover, and department stores were deluged with calls from interested customers. The next break came when she reluctantly agreed to do a licensing for her signature sweatshirt designs. Lacking the facilities to produce the line at a reasonable price, she signed an agreement with the Jones Apparel Group Inc. to manufacture them. The popularity of the sportswear is evident on streets throughout the world. Most recently, Kamali has entered the fields of shoes and children's clothing.

RICHARD LaMOTTA

A video engineer who attended law school at night, Richard LaMotta was always inventing various electronic gadgets that would allow him to go into business for himself, but he never had the money to market them. He was a man in search of an idea. "I was always looking for something that I could get into that could make me an entrepreneur."

His first experience with self-employment came when he opened a small ice-cream parlor with friends. At the shop, LaMotta was put in charge of research and development, the trail that would ultimately lead to Chipwich, the ice-cream sandwich novelty item. It was while scouting for products that LaMotta recalled an old passion: dunking.

A frenzied eight months and numerous pounds later, LaMotta had come up with a formula that allowed him to prepare and freeze a product that wouldn't turn soggy. A contest was held at the store to name the creation, and all that was left to do was to market it. Informed that it would cost $15 million to introduce it nationally, LaMotta determined to find a way to do it on his own for considerably less, for the $500,000 he had raised from savings and friends.

LaMotta's solution was to initiate a renaissance in street-cart vending. Not only was this the only way he could afford to market his product, but it also provided him with free advertising.

That was in 1981, the year LaMotta won best product awards along with Sony's Walkman and Rubik's Cube. Chipwich grew to employ 250 people, not including the 1500 commissioned vendors, and was sold in thirty U.S. cities and in markets abroad. In addition, the ice-cream sandwich is now also available in supermarkets and department stores. And although LaMotta has signed licensing agreements with Borden Inc., and others, he has lately experienced financial problems associated with expanding too quickly and ambitiously. He has cut back on his operation and is in the process of reorganizing the company.

GEORGE LANG

As George Lang is the first to admit, what he does depends upon whom you ask. To a patron of the charming Café des Artistes on Manhattan's West Side, he is a restaurant owner; to readers of *Travel & Leisure*, he is a magazine writer; to well-fed houseguests he is a magnificent cook; to hotel owners and developers he is a restaurant designer; to home cooks he is the author of the cookbook *Cuisine of Hungary*. And if you ask George Lang, he will answer that he is all of these, and add linguist (he speaks five languages), photographer, violinist, calligrapher, and, above all, innovator.

After emigrating from Hungary in 1946, he began his career as a page turner for musicians at Carnegie Hall (of which he is now a trustee), and later played violin in a symphony orchestra. Forgoing his career in music, he happened into a job in the kitchen of a New York City private club, and from that day on his work has involved food in one way or another. He worked his way up through various kitchen jobs until he ran the kitchen at the Waldorf-Astoria (where he planned dinners for Queen Elizabeth II and Princess Grace), and then took over management of the Four Seasons restaurant. Now he consults on new restaurants and other food-related projects for a fee estimated to be $3,500 per day.

"I thrive on variety," says Lang of his career and present status as consultant. Recent projects include food service for the King Cole Room at the St. Regis-Sheraton Hotel, the Museum of Modern Art, and the Citicorp Center, all in New York.

RICHARD LEIBNER

Richard Leibner and his job seem so suited to one another that it only makes sense that the job didn't really exist until Leibner invented it. Television news and Richard Leibner came of age at approximately the same time; television-news "talent agenting" became a field when Leibner began representing television-news talent. And the field first made news itself when Leibner engineered the deal whereby Dan Rather succeeded Walter Cronkite for a contract reported to be worth eight million dollars.

Leibner started out as a CPA, joining his father's firm after graduating from college with a degree in accounting. That, he believes, was a mistake ("You should never work for a parent. Period."), although it was the means by which he came to fill in at Nate Bienstock's insurance company, which was doing more and more work for the talent supplied to the nascent television-news industry. The work Leibner was doing at Bienstock's— clearing paychecks, accounting—wasn't a vast improvement over what he had been doing for his father, but the news aspect of the job began to intrigue him. "There was a list of thirty-five names—who were they? What did they look like? Who was Eric Sevareid? Winston Burdett? Lou Cioffi? Alexander Kendrick? Nate had a lot of the early best names."

Leibner spent the next several years working with Beinstock, and when Bienstock retired, the company became the exclusive domain of Leibner, as did the field of television-news talent agenting. Clients now include Morley Safer, Tom Jarriel, Ed Bradley, Morton Dean, and of course, Dan Rather.

DAVID LIEDERMAN

Since opening his first cookie shop in Manhattan in June 1979, David Liederman estimates that he has spent a total of twenty thousand dollars on advertising David's Cookies, and is now opening new stores at a rate of two each week, with over seventy shops around the country and abroad.

Liederman, a lawyer, trained at the Troisgros restaurant in Roanne—the first American to be accepted to work at the fabled French restaurant—and returned to the United States to practice law. That didn't last long, however; his true love, food, beckoned. After developing his first food product, Saucier, he received backing to introduce it nationally. "I had a very good track record out of France. I can be very convincing when it comes to food products, because the main thing I am is a consumer and eater. I eat everything. I eat too much. That's why I'm trying to get into a lettuce deal so I can taste lettuce instead of cookies."

Liederman was able to raise only $150,000 to promote Saucier, "a very esoteric, very upscale, very elegant, delicious sauce base," and the sum proved too small to educate the public to appreciate a product so esoteric and elegant. But it was while on the road for Saucier that Liederman came up with a product for which there was an existing market: cookies. His cookies have won almost every taste test they've been in, and are considered among the best on the market.

Liederman was so certain about his cookie scheme that he didn't hesitate to go into debt for half a million dollars to set up the first shop. His profits have risen steadily since then, and he has introduced David's Ice Cream as well.

The following is a recipe David offers for cookies almost as good as his own.

Butterscotch Chocolate-Chunk Cookies:
½ pound unsalted butter
½ pound brown sugar, well packed
½ teaspoon salt
½ teaspoon pure vanilla extract
1 large egg
8 ounces unbleached flour, by weight
8 ounces imported bittersweet chocolate, roughly chopped by hand

Preheat oven to 400 degrees. Combine all ingredients except flour and chocolate until smooth and lump-free, either by hand or with mixer at medium speed. Add flour and chocolate and mix only till traces of flour can be seen in the dough. Drop by teaspoonfuls two inches apart on a well-buttered sheet. Bake six to eight minutes or until edges barely begin to brown. Cool on wire rack.

EDWARD McCABE

One of Edward McCabe's most memorable advertising campaigns is the familiar series for Perdue chicken, featuring Frank Perdue and the slogan "It takes a tough man to make a tender chicken." That, however, is only one of the many noteworthy and successful campaigns originated by McCabe. His company, Scali, McCabe, Sloves, has also created ads for Volvo ("Fat cars die young") and the profitable SAS ("When an airline makes money, the passenger profits from it"). Not only has McCabe conceived and executed award-winning ad copy, but he has also had a hand in managing the rapid growth of his agency, recently purchased by Ogilvy & Mather, from a rank of 227 in world income in 1967 to 31 in 1984.

He started in the mail room. Told by an employment agency that he couldn't work anywhere but a factory because he didn't have a high-school diploma, McCabe lied about the diploma and got a job in an ad-agency mail room. Told by the agency he couldn't write ads because he lacked a college degree (after having already written several ads), he switched agencies and allowed his new employer to assume he had a degree. In 1967 he joined with two other men in a partnership that produced Scali, McCabe, Sloves, and became president.

He claims it was fear that drove him on: "I was afraid that if I didn't devote everything to it, they'd catch me and send me back to high school."

JERRY RUBIN

"I'm a connector, a catalyst," is how Jerry Rubin explains the continuity underlying his transitions from journalist (fifties) to revolutionary (sixties) to businessman (seventies) to "networker" (eighties). Rubin furthermore insists that he has been successful in each of these endeavors. Relentlessly cheerful and optimistic, he has gone from being a Yippie and federal defendant to a stockbroker (with the now-defunct John Muir Company) on Wall Street to entrepreneur and deal-cutter extraordinaire; or, as he prefers, *catalyst.*

Rubin's latest venture is the Business Networking Salon, an organization that provides opportunities for young professionals to meet one another, make contacts, exchange business cards, set up deals, dance, and drink—with Rubin clearing a profit by splitting the cover-charge proceeds with cohost Studio 54, New York's flagship discotheque.

Networking began in Rubin's Manhattan high-rise apartment, and was prompted by the confluence of two needs: to meet women after his wife had left him, and to meet potential investors and clients for his Wall Street interests. Invitations asked that recipients bring with them the most interesting person they knew, and guests left their business cards at the door. From these soirees came the idea that the arrangement could sustain itself as a business.

Always responsive to the currents of the times, Rubin explains, "Business is the activism of the eighties. The Networking thing is large, and that is the eighties. It's the new amalgam, and it starts with another principle. That men and women are equal." So career-conscious singles can have fun for profit, and work while they dance.

Never content to let an idea be, Rubin has initiated Business Networking 500 Club, a smaller, less social networking system organized on a "deal-making level" with a limited membership and dues. Rubin's stake in this one is a percentage of the take: For any deal consummated under the auspices of Networking 500, Rubin receives a commission.

JAN STUART

Jan Stuart is a son a mother can be truly proud of: Not only has he founded a successful business, but he did so by following her advice. It was at her suggestion that he entered the men's skin-care-product field, where, in just a few years' time, his products have come to compete with such established names as Estée Lauder's Aramis and Ralph Lauren's Polo.

After graduating from the University of Rhode Island, Stuart got a job as a sales representative in the garment center of New York—"and hated it," and then worked in advertising. All the while he was looking for an idea, a means by which he could make a name and fortune for himself. In 1979 his mother mentioned an article she had read in the newspaper predicting that men's fragrances and skin care would soon become a big business. "I laughed. I thought it was real funny." When he stopped laughing, Stuart realized that here was what he had been looking for: "something that nobody else did."

So with fifty thousand dollars and the aid of nutritionist Herbert Feldman, Stuart produced a line of skin-care products for men. They were not an immediate success. Unable to place his product in retail outlets or to afford conventional advertising, Stuart placed mail-order ads in men's, particularly gay men's, magazines, and focused on attracting the gay market.

Stuart moved out of his apartment and into the Ninety-second Street Y. His new address had the twin advantages of reduced rent (thirty-one dollars a week) and a test-marketing situation: There were hundreds of men there who shaved daily and were happy to respond to questions about his products.

In 1980 Bloomingdale's admitted Stuart to its vendors, and now the department store accounts for 25 percent of Stuart's sales. He has also placed his product in other department stores throughout the country.

CHRISTOPHER WHITTLE

Christopher Whittle and Phillip Moffitt began one of history's most successful publishing partnerships as undergraduates at the University of Tennessee in 1969. Their

13–30 Corporation (the name refers to the age spread of their original audience) now publishes sixteen magazines. The other Whittle-Moffitt venture is *Esquire* magazine, which the partners took over in 1979 with Whittle as publisher and Moffitt as editor. Currently, Whittle is chairman and Moffitt editor-in-chief and president of *Esquire*. Thirteen–Thirty is estimated to be a fifty-million-dollar corporation, and the two companies together employ about three hundred people.

Nutshell, the magazine with which the company was launched, came about when Moffitt and Whittle were running an orientation program for students entering the university. A magazine, they determined, would be the most efficient way to impart information. *Nutshell* was such a success that they began publishing it at every major university in the country, until they were publishing 115 different magazines.

With *Esquire,* Whittle and Moffitt have continued with the concept that was one of the keys to *Nutshell's* success: They publish for their peers. *Nutshell* is now staffed largely with younger people and college interns; *Esquire*'s market is the young but aging baby boomer. More than anything, their success is a lesson in partnership.

Whittle prefaces all his remarks in this book with the comment: "In talking about me, the important thing to know is that anything in relation to *Esquire* or this company has been a joint effort of my partner and me, and I would not want it to appear that I take individual credit because that would not be fair to what our partnership is. It has been a joint effort, and it should be perceived that way."

DR. RICHARD WINTER

In 1959 Dr. Richard Winter founded a health clinic that would provide a comprehensive medical examination for fifty dollars. During the first few rough months of operating the clinic he would frequently calculate his "survival time"—how long he could continue before having to go out and raise more money. In the thirteenth month of the clinic, with funds left for three more months of operation, Dr. Winter saw his first profit. Twenty-six years later, Executive Health Examiners has a full-time staff of five hundred, in addition to over six hundred associates in four hundred cities around the world. Its client list includes over twelve hundred corporate and government organizations.

The idea for the clinic came at a time when Dr. Winter was becoming restless with his private practice. It occurred to him that there was no place where an individual could go for a standardized physical examination and be treated graciously and charged a reasonable fee; hospitals were for sick people, and private physicians didn't have the facilities. So Dr. Winter bought and rented the necessary equipment, and determined to give his clients the best treatment available, both in terms of medical and of personal attention. Executive Health Examiners now offers 109 different examination "packages," and treats each patient like a guest, providing valets in the dressing room, personal attendants, and meal service. Ninety-three percent of the people who visit the clinic are corporate clients, and the cost of the standard examination is around three hundred dollars.

In 1982 Dr. Winter began publishing with McGraw-Hill a series of books entitled *Executive Health,* a field of medicine he has more or less invented. The books deal with nutrition, fitness, and stress as factors affecting the executive. The company has also formed a communications group that produces films, seminars, and workshops dealing with the same topics.

LOIS WYSE

At the age of seventeen Lois Wyse began working for her hometown newspaper, the Cleveland *Press,* with the goal of becoming a writer. Soon thereafter she began to work with her then husband, Marc Wyse, on an advertising shopping column, which she wrote and he sold. "Wise Buys by Lois" did so well for advertisers that it grew rapidly, "and before we knew it, we sort of backed into the advertising business." Wyse Advertising, Inc., which now generates eighty-six million dollars in billings annually, still maintains its office in Cleveland, and also has an office in New York, which is run by Lois. With the company ranked among the top one hundred U.S. agencies, Wyse employs 175 people.

With six-thousand dollars borrowed from Lois Wyse's father, the couple established themselves as a viable agency, with Lois heading the creative side and Marc selling. The debt was paid off in less than a year. One of the company's better-known campaigns is the Smucker's series, "With a name like Smucker's, it has to be good," the longest-running slogan in advertising history. In addition, Lois Wyse has continued to write and has published over forty-six books of poetry, fiction, nonfiction, and children's stories, most recently, *The Six-Figure Woman (And How to Be One).*

INDEX